HERO HeadQuarters
Where kids join forces with a God!

PRESCHOOL TEACHER
For teachers of three-, four-, and five-year-olds

Using This Book 2
Characteristics of Preschoolers 3
Preschool Resources 4
Decorating Resources 6

SESSION 1—Heroes Do the Unexpected! 7
SESSION 2—Heroes Take Action! 15
SESSION 3—Heroes Step Out on Faith! 23
SESSION 4—Heroes Save the Day! 31
SESSION 5—Heroes Stand for Truth! 39

HHQ Team: Edward Willis Group, Jonathan R. Willis Photography, Cheri McMurren, Elaina Meyers, Rosemary H. Mitchell, Standard Publishing Creative Services Team, The Tenfold Collective, Jennifer Root Wilger

PreSchool Teacher is published by Standard Publishing, Cincinnati, Ohio,
www.standardpub.com.
Copyright © 2009 by Standard Publishing. All rights reserved. Printed in the United States of America.

USING THIS BOOK

BIBLE MEMORY lists the verse kids will learn.

LIFE FOCUS is the main thought that preschoolers will learn and remember.

MATERIALS
Items needed for each activity.

QUICK STEP:
Activities that are easy to prepare and teach.

OPTION:
Optional activities are included in Steps 1 and 3.

BIBLE BACKGROUND helps the teacher prepare the lesson.

MAKE IT WORK FOR YOU!
- Use this material with learning centers. Set up activities at different stations within the room.
- Use this material with a team approach. Have different team members plan and lead specific activities in each of the four steps.
- Use this material with large or small groups. Select the activities that work best with your class size, available time, and facilities.
- Use any unused options for Sunday nights, weeknights, or weekday programming.

SESSION 1

Heroes do the UNEXPECTED!

BIBLE BACKGROUND

The young girl had been taken captive. She was taken to a foreign country where she was made a servant to the wife of a well-respected, national hero, Naaman. But Naaman had a terrible disease—leprosy—and no one knew how to cure it.

Instead of having hard feelings toward the people of the foreign land, the young girl wanted her mistress' husband to be cured. Back home in Israel, she had heard of miracles done by Elisha, the prophet. She trusted in Elisha's God and was confident that the prophet could even cure leprosy, so she told her mistress about him.

But when Naaman and his men went to Elisha's house, Elisha didn't even come out! He just sent out a servant with a message: "Go wash yourself seven times in the Jordan River." Naaman was insulted. How could Elisha cure leprosy without even coming out to talk to him? How could the Jordan River cure him? But Naaman's men convinced him to do as the prophet said. What could it hurt? On the seventh time, Naaman's flesh became like that of a child, and Naaman was healed.

How grateful Naaman must have been to a kind servant girl who did the unexpected. Let's look for opportunities to offer unexpected kindness and perhaps point others to God!

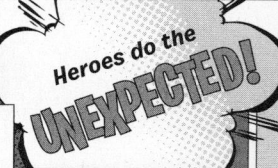

BIBLE STORY
A servant girl speaks up, and God's power heals Naaman (2 Kings 5:1-14).

BIBLE MEMORY
1 Timothy 4:12

Step 1	Step 2	Step 3	Step 4
Use one or more of these activities to help children *explore what it means to live the life of a servant.*	Use this interactive story to help children *tell what the servant girl did that was surprising.*	Use one or more of these activities to help children *identify ways they can be kind to others.*	Use this activity to help each child *choose a way to be a hero who is kind to someone.*
QUICK Step: Servant Says **Materials:** none	**Bible Story:** **Materials:** Bible; Teaching Resources Sheet 1, Sheet 6, and CD; glue or tape; jumbo craft sticks	**QUICK Step:** Be Kind **Materials:** Hero Handbook and stickers, crayons, pillowcase, classroom items	**QUICK Step:** "If Only" **Materials:** Teaching Resources CD, CD player
Option 1: Servant's Day **Materials:** bedding items	**Bible Review:** **Materials:** white or red dot stickers, washcloths or wet wipes	**Option 1:** Wash Dishes **Materials:** water table or plastic tub, water, dish soap, dishcloth, plastic dishes, towels, rubber gloves	
Option 2: Servant Snack **Materials:** water, pitchers, paper cups, fish-shaped crackers, dry cereal, raisins, large bowl, large spoons, napkins, wet wipes	**Bible Memory:** **Materials:** Teaching Resources Sheet 7 and CD, mini stickers	**Option 2:** If You're Kind and You Know It **Materials:** cleaning supplies	

STEP 1: Kids will be introduced to the theme and life focus.

STEP 2: Kids will hear the Bible story and interact with the Scripture passage.

STEP 3: Kids will discover how the Scripture applies to their lives.

STEP 4: Kids will commit to a personal action in response to what they've learned that day.

CHARACTERISTICS OF PRESCHOOLERS

Get to know the children in your class. Observe them, talk to them, listen to them, and read about them.

PHYSICALLY, PRESCHOOL CHILDREN
- can't sit still.
- need a lot of physical play and space to move around.
- are developing eye-to-hand coordination.

INTELLECTUALLY, PRESCHOOL CHILDREN
- have unlimited questions, especially "Why?"
- learn by experience and by using the five senses.
- think literally and do not understand abstracts.

EMOTIONALLY, PRESCHOOL CHILDREN
- are generally self-centered, but naturally loving.
- are determined and shouldn't be discouraged.
- have rapidly changing emotions.

SOCIALLY, PRESCHOOL CHILDREN
- imitate others, so good examples are important.
- are uninhibited and need protection.
- play side by side, but not always in cooperation with others.

SPIRITUALLY, PRESCHOOL CHILDREN
- are learning what God did and who Jesus is.
- know the Bible is a special book about God and Jesus.
- understand that prayer is talking to God and God listens to their prayers.

PreSchool Teacher

PRESCHOOL RESOURCES

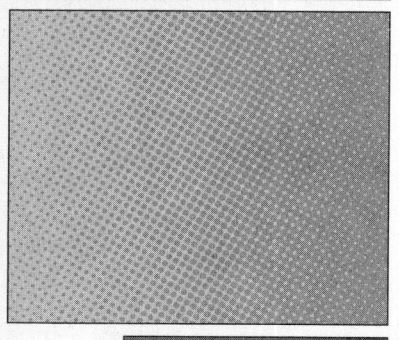

PRESCHOOL TEACHING RESOURCES

Don't miss this valuable resource! *PreSchool Teaching Resources* (020901210) is designed to expand and enhance your daily sessions. It offers a variety of additional activities and materials perfectly integrated into each day's session.

This packet includes the following 19" x 25" full-color sheets:

- A Servant Girl Speaks Up poster
- Shepherds Tell About Jesus poster
- An Army Officer Goes to Jesus poster
- A Boy Shares His Food poster
- A Young Man Shows Courage poster
- A Servant Girl Speaks Up story figures
- Bible Memory activity poster

In addition, you'll get a CD filled with unique and interactive materials, such as:

- Bible Memory activities
- Session-related activities
- "Stand Up!"—song especially for preschoolers
- Coloring pages
- Puzzle pages
- Hero HeadQuarters Family Pages
- Interactive Bible story music activities, action rhymes, and more

PRESCHOOL HERO HANDBOOK

Bring it all together with *PreSchool Hero Handbook* (020903010) designed just for preschoolers! This full-color, comic-book style resource will grab kids' attention and draw them in to fun activities and Bible reviews. Filled with a variety of learning tools, the *PreSchool Hero Handbook* will be a tremendous resource for you as you teach and reach kids for God.

PRESCHOOL RESOURCES

Here's some of what you'll find:

- fun, interactive Bible review
- application activities
- modern-day hero stories
- activity place mat
- "I Can Be a Hero" service cards
- stickers

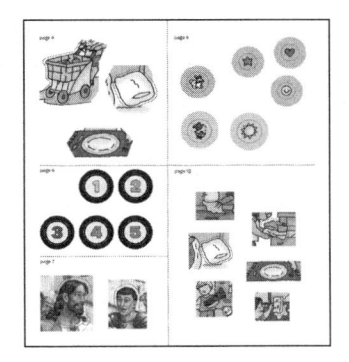

COOPER AND COOPER SKITS CD

Super Cooper to the rescue! Cooper (020903610) returns to entertain and teach the littlest heroes at Hero HQ! *Cooper Skits CD* (020904110) has five audio and five printable puppet skits, instructions for how to make his cape, and instructions to make his own stage. Use these skits during snack time, winding-down time, anytime to have Cooper help preschoolers understand how important it is to be a hero, no matter where they are!

HAPPY DAY® 5-BOOK SET

Each book from the *Happy Day® 5-Book Set* (020909010) will remind kids of the amazing Bible heroes! Includes *Old Testament Faith Heroes*, *The Story of Christmas*, *New Testament Faith Heroes*, *Five Small Loaves and Two Small Fish*, and *Paul's Great Adventures*. Read these to your students or give them as special gifts!

HAPPY DAY® DIGITAL BOOK BUNDLE

Children have enjoyed reading Happy Day® books for years. Now with *Happy Day® Digital Book Bundle* (020908910) you can show and tell the Bible stories again and again on the big screen using your computer and this NEW resource especially for the youngest heroes! Includes the five *Happy Day® 5-Book Set* and a Flash adaptation of each book. Your preschoolers will enjoy interacting with each day's Bible story in fun, new ways!

PreSchool Teacher

DECORATING RESOURCES

Transforming any room into a Hero HeadQuarters just right for preschoolers is easy with these simple and creative decorating ideas.

The *Decorating Pack* (020908310) contains 39" x 55" full-color sheets picturing Maintenance Mac, Water Woman, Pizza Man, and Cooper—the characters your kids will encounter each day at Hero HeadQuarters! Display the sheets on your wall or mount them as stand-up figures. You will also find a Bible Memory burst, five silhouettes (in color), a big logo, and an HHQ logo.

Take it a step further with the *Theme Pack* (020900510)! In addition to everything you get in the *Decorating Pack*, this resource also contains a *Giant Hero Backdrop* (9' wide!), a set of *Power Bursts,* and a Theme Pack Guide.

A variety of poster packs, *Life Focus Poster Pack* (020902410), *Site Names Poster Pack* (020902510), and *Bible Memory Poster Packs* (020902710 or 020902810), have been created to help you decorate and educate at Hero HeadQuarters. These posters are printed on 19" x 27" sheets.

And after you've set the environment with our resources, add some of your own! Build a tunnel out of a refrigerator box, leading from the outside of the classroom into the classroom. Place the beginning of the tunnel at the entrance of the classroom door. Display the Hero HeadQuarters logo above it. Kids will enjoy coming and going each day. Stretch colorful plastic party springs (purchased at department stores) into quirky designs and suspend from the ceiling among clouds found on the *Art & Decorating CD* (020902310). Using colored mural paper, make silhouettes of your kids to display among the silhouettes provided in the *Decorating Pack*. Attach a helium balloon on a string to each silhouette. Make your space look as much like or as different from the Hero HQ area as you'd like. The choice is yours and the possibilities are endless!

SESSION 1

Heroes do the UNEXPECTED!

BIBLE BACKGROUND

The young girl had been taken captive. She was taken to a foreign country where she was made a servant to the wife of a well-respected, national hero, Naaman. But Naaman had a terrible disease—leprosy—and no one knew how to cure it.

Instead of having hard feelings toward the people of the foreign land, the young girl wanted her mistress' husband to be cured. Back home in Israel, she had heard of miracles done by Elisha, the prophet. She trusted in Elisha's God and was confident that the prophet could even cure leprosy, so she told her mistress about him.

But when Naaman and his men went to Elisha's house, Elisha didn't even come out! He just sent out a servant with a message: "Go wash yourself seven times in the Jordan River." Naaman was insulted. How could Elisha cure leprosy without even coming out to talk to him? How could the Jordan River cure him? But Naaman's men convinced him to do as the prophet said. What could it hurt? On the seventh time, Naaman's flesh became like that of a child, and Naaman was healed.

How grateful Naaman must have been to a kind servant girl who did the unexpected. Let's look for opportunities to offer unexpected kindness and perhaps point others to God!

BIBLE STORY
A servant girl speaks up, and God's power heals Naaman (2 Kings 5:1-14).

BIBLE MEMORY
1 Timothy 4:12

Step 1	Step 2	Step 3	Step 4
Use one or more of these activities to help children *explore what it means to live the life of a servant.*	Use this interactive story to help children *tell what the servant girl did that was surprising.*	Use one or more of these activities to help children *identify ways they can be kind to others.*	Use this activity to help each child *choose a way to be a hero who is kind to someone.*
QUICK Step: Servant Says **Materials:** none	**Bible Story:** **Materials:** Bible; *Teaching Resources* Sheet 1, Sheet 6, and CD; glue or tape; jumbo craft sticks	**QUICK Step:** Be Kind **Materials:** *Hero Handbook* and stickers, crayons, pillowcase, classroom items	**QUICK Step:** "If Only" **Materials:** *Teaching Resources* CD, CD player
Option 1: Servant's Day **Materials:** bedding items	**Bible Review:** **Materials:** white or red dot stickers, washcloths or wet wipes	**Option 1:** Wash Dishes **Materials:** water table or plastic tub, water, dish soap, dishcloth, plastic dishes, towels, rubber gloves	
Option 2: Servant Snack **Materials:** water, pitchers, paper cups, fish-shaped crackers, dry cereal, raisins, large bowl, large spoons, napkins, wet wipes	**Bible Memory:** **Materials:** *Teaching Resources* Sheet 7 and CD, mini stickers	**Option 2:** If You're Kind and You Know It **Materials:** cleaning supplies	

PreSchool Teacher 7

LIFE FOCUS: Heroes do the UNEXPECTED!

SESSION 1

MATERIALS
none

MATERIALS
bedding items

STEP 1
Use one or more of these activities to help children *explore what it means to live the life of a servant.*

QUICK STEP: SERVANT SAYS

During VBS we are going to learn how we can be heroes used by God to do wonderful things and make a difference in the lives of people around us! Today we are going to learn about how God used a young servant girl. We don't know her name, but she spoke up and God's power healed Naaman. You can speak up for God too!

I'm going to choose one person to be the servant. The servant will speak up and tell us an action to do, then lead us in doing that action seven times. You can clap seven times, hop seven times, or spin seven times—don't get dizzy! Or you can lead us in doing something that a servant does, like sweeping the floor or making the beds. Whatever you choose, do it seven times. Then the next friend will have a turn. Everyone will get a turn to be the servant.

Choose a child to begin the game and have the children count along with you. Some children may need encouragement or a suggestion. Don't worry if an action is repeated several times.

Why do you think we are doing all of our servant actions seven times? Listen carefully to our story, and you'll find out!

ESPECIALLY FOR 3s!
Most 3s will need suggestions. As each child leads, suggest two actions and let him choose.

OPTION 1: SERVANT'S DAY

During VBS we are going to learn how we can be heroes used by God to do wonderful things and make a difference in the lives of people around us! **Can you tell me what kind of jobs servants do?** (wash dishes, sweep floors, make beds) Show children the bedding materials. **Servants do jobs around the house to help their masters. They might cook, or clean, or make the beds. In Bible times most people had beds on the floor. Let's pretend we're servants and make some beds right now.**

As you help children make the beds, talk with them about the life of a servant. Include questions, such as:

• **Do you like making your bed? What would it be like to make beds for everyone in your house?**

• **Do you think servants make their own beds in the morning too?**

• **Would you like to be a servant and make everyone's beds?**

We don't know her name, but the servant girl in our Bible story today worked very hard. One day she did a special job to help her sick master get well. And because she did that special job, she is today's Bible hero. Our Bible story will tell us more about that.

OPTION 2: SERVANT SNACK

Talk with children about the kinds of jobs servants do. Explain that servants often prepare food for the members of their household. Tell children that today they will practice being servants by preparing food for one another.

Have all the "servants" wash their hands or use wet wipes. Form two groups. Assign a teacher or helper to each group. Have one group prepare the snack by mixing together the raisins, cereal, and crackers in a large bowl. Have the other group pour water from small pitchers into cups and set the table with napkins.

When the snack is ready and the table is set, invite everyone to sit down to eat. Encourage children to use their manners and remind them to say thank you to the people who have served them. Before eating, lead children in a simple, familiar prayer.

As children eat, talk with them about the experience of preparing food for others. Ask questions, such as:
- **How do you feel after doing all that work?**
- **Are you happy when you serve your friends?**
- **Are you tired from all that stirring and pouring?**

Let children respond, then hold up a glass of water. **This water reminds me of the hero in today's Bible story. Listen and see what happens when a servant girl's master visits a river.**

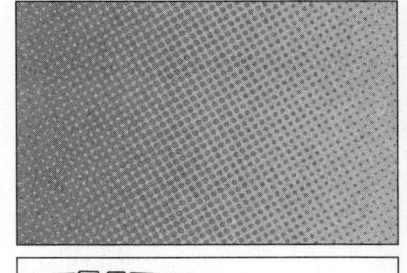

MATERIALS

water, pitchers, paper cups, fish-shaped crackers, dry cereal, raisins, large bowl, large spoons, napkins, wet wipes

TEACHING TIPS

If your kids travel to the Super Snacks site for their snacks, you may want to choose another activity instead of Servant Snack.

Be aware of food allergies when providing snacks for preschoolers. Provide alternate foods and drinks as needed.

LIFE FOCUS: Heroes do the UNEXPECTED!

SESSION 1

MATERIALS

Bible; *Teaching Resources* Sheet 1, Sheet 6 figures 1a–1f and water scene, and CD Session 1 Elisha's House printable file; glue or tape; jumbo craft sticks

BEFORE CLASS

Display Sheet 1 in story area. Remove the figures and water scene from Sheet 6. Laminate the figures if desired. Glue or tape each figure to a jumbo craft stick. The Naaman figure is two-sided, so place the craft stick in between before taping together. Print out Elisha's house from the CD and post it at children's eye level outside the story area. Perforate the slit in the water scene and post near Elisha's house, taping only the top half of the scene.

TEACHING TIP

Introduce the story of the servant girl using *Old Testament Faith Heroes* from the *Happy Day® 5-Book Set* or *Happy Day® Digital Book Bundle*. This will calm down the children to be ready to participate in the Bible story.

STEP 2
Use this interactive story to help kids *tell what the servant girl did that was surprising.*

BIBLE STORY: A SERVANT GIRL SPEAKS UP, AND GOD'S POWER HEALS NAAMAN

Open the Bible to 2 Kings 5 and place it on your lap. **Today our Bible story hero is a young servant girl. Do we know her name?** *(No.)* **This young girl was taken from her home to serve the wife of a man named Naaman.**

What does a servant do? *(Mention jobs children performed in Step 1.)* How do you think the girl felt about leaving her family to be a servant?

Well, Naaman had a very bad skin disease and no one knew how to make it better. Scratch your arms if you've ever had a bug bite, or something itchy on your skin. How did it feel? Naaman's skin felt even worse!

(Hold up servant girl 1a with Naaman's wife 1b. Move figures as if talking.) Naaman's wife and the servant girl were talking about Naaman. The girl was *so* sad to hear that news. But then she had an idea! The girl said, "If only Naaman could go see a man named Elisha. He could make Naaman well again."

Well, it was a long way to see Elisha, but guess what? Naaman started out on his trip. *(Hold up Naaman 1c, leprosy side).* He took some servants with him. Let's pretend we're Naaman's servants. *(Hold up servants 1d).* Find a partner and hold hands. It's a long way. *(Lead children around the room, talking about what it might have been like to travel by foot. End your journey at Elisha's house.)*

Whew! Naaman and his servants were so tired. They probably couldn't wait to see Elisha. But guess what? *(Choose four children, giving each one of the following: Naaman, servants, Elisha 1e, and Elisha's servant 1f. Place the two children holding Naaman and servants on one side of the house and the other two children on the other side. Help children move figures along with the story.)*

Naaman's servants knocked on the door of Elisha's house. *(Have Naaman's men knock on the house.)* They knocked and they knocked, but Elisha didn't answer. He just stayed in his house. Finally Elisha sent his servant out. *(Have Elisha's servant cross over to Naaman's side of the house.)*

Elisha's servant told Naaman that Elisha said that if Naaman wanted to get better, he had to go wash himself in the river seven times. Huh? Naaman was supposed to get better by taking a bath? Have you ever heard of that?

Naaman was confused. Why did he have to make this long trip just to wash himself in a river? Why couldn't he wash himself in a river closer to his home? Why didn't Elisha come out of his house? And why did Elisha's servant say he had to wash one-two-three-four-five-six-seven times?

But Naaman's servants said, "Why don't you try it?" What do you think? If someone told you to do this, would you? *(Let kids respond.)*

(Insert Naaman in the blue water, moving him up and down with each

count.) Naaman decided to do what Elisha told him to do. He washed one . . . two . . . three . . . four . . . five . . . six . . . seven times. When he came up the seventh time, the spots were gone! *(Turn Naaman around on the seventh count.)* No more itching and scratching! Naaman felt great. Show me what you do when you feel great. *(Encourage children to jump for joy. Collect all figures from children.)*

(Show each figure when mentioned.) Naaman felt great because his skin disease was gone. He listened to his *servants,* who listened to *Elisha's servant,* who listened to *Elisha,* God's special helper. Naaman also listened to his *wife,* who listened to her *servant girl.* God did a great thing for Naaman, and it started with one little girl. Let's clap our hands and shout, "Yay, God!" *(Do so.)* Naaman was healed and believed in God because one little girl spoke up. We can speak up for God too!

BIBLE REVIEW

Naaman's skin was covered with spots because he had a bad skin disease. Let's use these stickers to make our skin look like Naaman's. Give each child stickers for each arm. **What did Elisha's servant tell Naaman to do?** Review how Naaman followed Elisha's instructions to wash seven times in the river.

Say the following chant, then repeat it with the children:

**The servant girl said, "Go see God's man!
If he can't help you, no one can."**

Now count with me, and while we're counting, "wash" the spots off. Give each child a washcloth to wash the stickers off as you continue the chant.

**1-2-3-4-5-6-7—we trust Elisha's God in Heaven.
7-6-5-4-3-2-1—we wash, wash, wash, now we're all done.**

BIBLE MEMORY

Using the Bible Memory poster, introduce the Bible Memory. Show the four sections and explain that you'll be adding stickers to the poster when you see young heroes setting good examples by saying kind words, doing loving actions, trusting God, or thinking pure thoughts.

Lead children in saying the verse phrase by phrase using the Bible Memory Actions. After you review the verse, talk about how the verse relates to the Bible story. **Even though the servant girl in our story was young, she did a surprising and brave thing. She knew God could heal Naaman, and she wasn't afraid to talk about that. We can use our words to talk about God too.**

STORY OPTION

Instead of moving the kids around the room, put the figures in a sand pan, changing the background scene when needed.

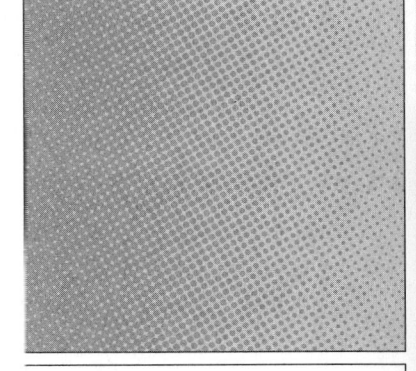

MATERIALS

white or red dot stickers, washcloths or wet wipes

TEACHING TIP

Children might enjoy marching and singing "Naaman Was Sick" found on the resources CD Session 1 printable file.

MATERIALS

Teaching Resources Sheet 7 and CD All Sessions Bible Memory Actions *(NIV* or *KJV)* printable file, mini stickers

TEACHING TIPS

We suggest *Heart of Gold Micro-Mini* (43123)—252 stickers in a pack!

After the children have learned a portion of the Bible Memory, play the Right on Target game found on the resources CD.

SESSION 1

PreSchool Teacher **11**

LIFE FOCUS: Heroes do the UNEXPECTED!

SESSION 1

MATERIALS
Hero Handbook pp. 3 and 4 and stickers, crayons, pillowcase, classroom items

MATERIALS
water table or plastic tub, water, dish soap, dishcloth, plastic dishes, towels, rubber gloves

COOPER SKIT OPTION
Kids will enjoy watching Cooper as he does something totally unexpected in today's skit. He wants to surprise the leader, but it turns out that the surprise is on him! You can find the audio skit and printable file on *Cooper Skits CD*.

STEP 3
Use one or more of these activities to help children *identify ways they can be kind to others.*

QUICK STEP: BE KIND

Show children the pictures in the *Hero Handbook* page 4. Talk about how the children in each picture are heroes because they are being kind. Help children match the stickers to the ways they will be heroes. They can choose ways they already help at home, or new ways they'd like to try this week.

Before class, place several classroom items in a pillowcase, such as a box of crayons, a baby doll, or a book. Let each child take a turn selecting an item from the pillowcase and show a way he will use that item to be kind to someone. Examples: draw a picture for someone who is sick, give a doll to a child who doesn't have one.

If time allows, have children look at the Bible story picture on page 3 of their handbooks. Encourage children to retell the story as they color the picture. Discuss the questions and encourage children to tell about times they've spoken up to help others.

OPTION 1: WASH DISHES

Say, **Today we learned about how a servant girl was a hero because she was kind to someone who needed help. God wants us to be heroes and be kind to others who need our help. Let's practice one way we can be kind at home.**

Have children explore what it feels like to wash dishes. Talk about the water, soap, and the rubber gloves. As you wash dishes with the children, use the following questions to talk with them about ways they can be heroes by being kind helpers at home.

- **How do you get the dishes clean at your house?**
- **How do you think they got the dishes clean at the servant girl's house?**
- **What ways do you help at home?**
- **What does it feel like to be a kind helper?**

OPTION 2: IF YOU'RE KIND AND YOU KNOW IT

The servant girl in our story today was a hero because she was kind to Naaman. One way we can be heroes is by helping to keep our room clean. While we clean our room, let's sing a song about some other ways we can be heroes. I think you might know this tune. Maybe you'll find some ways you can be kind!

Lead the children in singing as they clean the room. Encourage them to clean the tables and chairs using the spray bottles filled with water and then wiping with the paper towels. Have other children dust shelves. Invite other children to sweep the floor and pick up trash. After the children have finished their tasks, praise them for being heroes who help keep the classroom clean.

(tune: If You're Happy and You Know It)
If you're kind and you know it, share your toys. *(pass a toy around)*
If you're kind and you know it, share your toys.
If you're kind and you know it, then your face will surely show it.
If you're kind and you know it, share your toys.

More verses:
If you're kind and you know it, make your bed. *(pretend to pull up a blanket)*
If you're kind and you know it, share God's love. *(hug a friend)*
If you're kind and you know it, share a smile. *(turn to a friend and smile)*
If you're kind and you know it, say "Amen!" *(pump hand up in the air)*

MATERIALS

cleaning supplies (e.g., dust cloths, spray bottles, paper towels, disposable dusters, small brooms, dustpans)

TEACHING TIP

Kids may just want to sing, using the motions found in the song.

LIFE FOCUS: Heroes do the UNEXPECTED!

MATERIALS

Teaching Resources CD Track 1 and CD All Sessions "Stand Up!" printable file, CD player

For more fun, have your kids visit these sites (or use the leader's guides):
- **Power Projects**—Choose from creative and purposeful projects that will help kids remember to be heroes who do the unexpected for God!
- **Super Snacks**—Kids will love making and eating these tasty snacks that reinforce the Bible story!
- **Action Games**—Give kids time to move, play, work on hero skills, and relax. All the super fun activities connect to the Bible hero story and Bible focus.

SESSION 1

STEP 4
Use this activity to help each child *choose a way to be a hero who is kind to someone.*

QUICKSTEP: "IF ONLY"

Play this fun game in the style of Simon Says to help children step up and be kind.

In our Bible story, the servant girl told Naaman's wife, "If only Naaman could see Elisha, God's special helper, I know he would be healed." The Bible tells us that because the servant girl decided to act like a hero and speak up, God healed Naaman's sickness. Listen to these "If onlys." If you hear me say a way you can be a hero, step right up to show you'll do it!

If only you could set the table, take seven giant steps.

If only you could ask a friend to play, hop seven times.

If only you could pick up your toys, take seven baby steps.

If only you could bring a friend to VBS, turn around seven times.

If only you could hug someone who is sad, hug seven friends right now.

Invite children to give you additional suggestions. Then ask children for ideas of ways they can be heroes for God by being kind to others.

Close by praying, **Dear God, thanks for the example of the servant girl. Even though we are young, help us to be heroes and speak up and show Your kindness to our friends and family. In Jesus' name, amen.**

Close the session by teaching the song "Stand Up!" to the kids. The song and lyrics can be found on the resources CD.

From the *PreSchool Teaching Resources CD* Session 1 printable file
- Add your own news or leave as is and print copies of the **Hero HeadQuarters Family Page**. It lets parents know what their kids are learning and gives an overview of the Bible story, as well as suggests ways they can encourage their children to be heroes, doing the unexpected!
- Print copies of **A Servant Girl Speaks Up Puzzle** onto card stock. Kids will love making puzzles to take home. Have a supply of envelopes handy for them to put their puzzle pieces in.
- Print copies of **A Servant Girl Speaks Up Coloring Page** for kids to take home and color with their friends and families.

SESSION 2

Heroes take ACTION!

BIBLE BACKGROUND

As explained in Luke 1, Mary's pregnancy before she married Joseph came from God's action. With child by God's Holy Spirit, Mary had already heard that her child would be called the Son of the Highest (v. 32).

While with Joseph in his ancestral town of Bethlehem for the census, Mary gave birth to her baby. The manger in which she put Him most likely was a feedbox. God's Son came into His world in humble circumstances.

The visitors that came to see the baby came from humble classes also. Some shepherds out in the pasture watching their flocks received the first birth announcement along with some confirming signs from an unlikely source—God's angels.

The shepherds went swiftly to Bethlehem. There was the baby in the manger, with Joseph and Mary watching Him. Can you imagine how eagerly those men told Mary and Joseph about the light that had startled them? about the angel and his message? about the choir singing of the glory in Heaven and peace on earth? It must have been wonderful! Never would Mary forget the story of the shepherds. Neither would the people who heard the shepherds tell that story over and over.

And we won't forget either! That baby is our Savior and our Lord. So who can you tell?

BIBLE STORY
Shepherds see baby Jesus and tell everyone about the Savior (Luke 2:1-20).

BIBLE MEMORY
1 Timothy 4:12

Step 1	Step 2	Step 3	Step 4
Use one or more of these activities to help children *explore the life of a shepherd*.	Use this interactive story to help children *tell what action the shepherds took after they saw Jesus*.	Use one or more of these activities to help children *identify ways they can tell others about Jesus*.	Use this activity to help each child *choose a way to be a hero who tells about Jesus*.
QUICK Step: *Baa Baa*, Shepherd **Materials:** none	**Bible Story: ** **Materials:** Bible, *Teaching Resources* Sheet 2 and CD, storytelling items (see p. 18), CD player	**QUICK Step:** Who Will I Tell? **Materials:** *Hero Handbook* and stickers	**QUICK Step:** Announcing... Jesus! **Materials:** *Teaching Resources CD*, washable markers or crayons, CD player
Option 1: Shepherd Head Coverings **Materials:** fabric squares, yarn	**Bible Review:** **Materials:** none	**Option 1:** We Can Go! **Materials:** none	
Option 2: Shepherd's Supper **Materials:** pita bread; dried fruit; whipped cream cheese, hummus, and yogurt; plastic spoons; cups; napkins; plates; wet wipes	**Bible Memory:** **Materials:** *Teaching Resources* Sheet 7 and CD, mini stickers	**Option 2:** Got to Tell Somebody! **Materials:** 12-oz plastic cups, *Teaching Resources CD*, yarn or string, scissors, washable markers or crayons, glue, small paper clips	

PreSchool Teacher 15

LIFE FOCUS: Heroes take ACTION!

MATERIALS
none

TEACHING TIP
You can reinforce basic preschool skills as you form groups. Group children by type or color of clothing. For example, you might have all the children wearing sandals form one group and the children wearing lace-up shoes form another group. For this game, it's okay if the groups aren't the same size. Think about shepherds and sheep!

MATERIALS
fabric squares, yarn
(optional: washable markers)

TEACHING TIP
If your church has Bible-time costumes, you may want to add robes, staffs, or other items for shepherd dress-up.

STEP 1 — Use one or more of these activities to help children *explore the life of a shepherd.*

QUICK STEP: BAA BAA, SHEPHERD

Today we are going to explore the life of a shepherd. Shepherds take care of sheep. They help the sheep find food and water and protect the sheep from danger. Let's play a game to find out more about that. Our game will have sheep and shepherds. You will all get a chance to be both a sheep and a shepherd.

Form two groups—shepherds and sheep. Have the shepherds form a circle around the sheep. Explain that the shepherds will try to keep the sheep in the "pen." The sheep will crawl around on hands and knees and try to wander out. Have the shepherds try to gently lead the sheep across the room to "green grass and water." When most of the children have crossed the room, have the groups switch roles and travel back across the "field" in the same way.

After each group has a turn to be shepherds and sheep, talk with children about the game.

• **What was it like to be a shepherd? Were the sheep noisy? Did the sheep follow where you were leading them?**

• **Did you like being a shepherd or a sheep? Why?**

• **When you were sheep, did you wonder where the shepherds were taking you? Did you trust the shepherds? Why or why not?**

It's a big job to take care of sheep! They need food and water, and sometimes they wander away. Our heroes in today's Bible story are some shepherds who got a special surprise one night while they were watching their sheep.

ESPECIALLY FOR 3s!
Have the adult and teen leaders be the shepherds who guide the sheep (children) to various areas of the room.

OPTION 1: SHEPHERD HEAD COVERINGS

Give each child a fabric square. Show children how to fringe the square's edges by pulling on the loose strings. If time allows, let children decorate the squares with markers.

As children finish their squares, help them put on the head coverings. Position the finished square over the child's head. Line one side up with the child's eyebrows so that the child can still see. The rest of the square will hang behind the child's head to keep the sun and bugs off—just like a real shepherd! Wrap the yarn around the child's head at eyebrow level and tie in back. Let extra

yarn hang down in back. Talk with children about a shepherd's clothing and life.
- **Why do you think shepherds wore robes and head coverings?**
- **What do you think shepherds ate? How do you think they cooked their food?**
- **Where do you think shepherds slept?**

Shepherds spent long days taking care of their sheep. I'm sure they were tired at nighttime! Our heroes in today's Bible story are some shepherds who had an unusual nighttime visitor.

OPTION 2: SHEPHERD'S SUPPER

Have children wash their hands or use wet wipes. Set out the pita, dried fruit, and toppings. Let children choose what fillings to put in their pita. As children enjoy the snack, talk with them about what shepherds might eat.
- **Where do you think shepherds get their food?**
- **What kind of dishes do you think shepherds use? Where do you think they keep the food and dishes while they are out with the sheep?**
- **How do you think shepherds wash their hands? How do they clean their dishes?**

Encourage children to be creative in asking questions and imagining what it would be like to live as shepherds.

MATERIALS

wet wipes; pita bread; dried fruit; whipped cream cheese, hummus, and yogurt; plastic spoons; cups; napkins; plates

TEACHING TIPS

If your kids travel to the Super Snacks site for their snacks, you may want to choose another activity instead of the Shepherd's Supper.

If you choose, children can prepare their snacks now and enjoy them during the Bible story as you sit around the shepherds' "campfire."

Remember to check all food allergies. Have jelly available for those with dairy allergies.

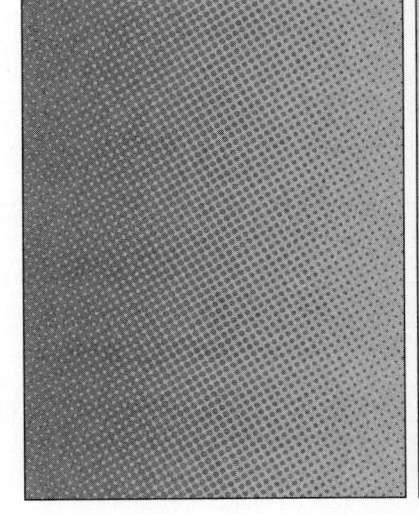

PreSchool Teacher

LIFE FOCUS: Heroes take ACTION!

MATERIALS

Bible, blocks, tissue paper, red cellophane, flashlight, angel outfit, blankets, *Teaching Resources* Sheet 2 and CD Session 2 nativity scene, CD player, CD of "Hallelujah" chorus

BEFORE CLASS

Display Sheet 2 in story area. Set up a campfire using wooden blocks, tissue paper, and red cellophane. Lay blankets near the campfire. Post the nativity picture scene in an out-of-the way place.

Arrange for a teen or an adult to appear as the angel. Give her the flashlight and a copy of the story script. Practice the appearance before the children arrive.

TEACHING TIP

If you have the snack during the story, have children clean their hands, then distribute the snack while sitting around the campfire. When you pray, don't forget to thank God for the safety of the sheep, just as the shepherds would!

STEP 2 — Use this interactive story to help children *tell what action the shepherds took after they saw Jesus.*

BIBLE STORY: SHEPHERDS SEE BABY JESUS AND TELL EVERYONE ABOUT THE SAVIOR

Have children sit on the blankets. If you made the head coverings in Step 1, have children wear them. Open the Bible to Luke 2 and place it on your lap.

I'd like to tell you one of my favorite stories from the Bible! I want you to imagine you're one of the shepherds who was there the night this special story happened. Huddle close because it was a dark, cold, quiet night.

It had been a long day for the shepherds. Finally, they counted the last of the sheep. Count with me: 1 *(baa)*, 2 *(baa)*, 3 *(continue up to 10)*.

Shepherds, I'm tired! We followed the sheep up the hill and down the hill and through the trees. I'm so glad we didn't lose any sheep. I think it would be safe to close our eyes for just a little while, don't you? Close your eyes with me.

Everybody stretch and yawn, then lie down and close your eyes. *(In a sing-song voice)* Sleeping, sleeping, all the shepherds sleeping . . . now I lay me down to sleep, I pray the Lord my sheep to keep . . . sleeping, sleeping, all the shepherds sleeping. *(Pat each child's back as if you were soothing him or her to sleep.)*

Just as the sleepy shepherds were closing their eyes, a bright light appeared! Shepherds, open your eyes! What could it be? I'm scared!

(Have the angel appear and shine the flashlight and say,) "Do not be afraid. I am here to bring you good news of great joy. Today in the town of Bethlehem a Savior, who is Christ the Lord, has been born. You will find the baby wrapped in cloths, lying in a manger." *(Turn off flashlight, angel turns around.)*

(Look at the children and raise your hands, as if very confused.) Huh?! Good news . . . great joy . . . and a baby? What do you think it could mean?

Then suddenly *(angel turns back around, flashlight on, angelic music plays)* there were hundreds of angels singing and saying "Glory to God in the highest, and on earth peace, goodwill toward men." *(Angel exits, music stops.)*

Well, what do you think we should do, shepherds? I've never seen anything like that before! Should we tell somebody? Do you think anyone will believe us? Shepherds, I say we tell somebody. Let's go to Bethlehem and see this baby Jesus.

(Lead children on a hunt for the nativity picture. Start out walking, then increase your pace until you find it.) Look! There's baby Jesus, just like the angels said! That must be His mother and father. Baby Jesus is lying in the manger all right. God's own Son, and we're here to see Him! I can hardly believe it! Let's go and tell everybody!

(Cup your hands over your mouth and call out repeatedly, "Jesus, God's Son is born!" as you lead the children back to the campfire area. Encourage children to join you in shouting out the good news! Back at the campfire, ask children)

SESSION 2

18 HERO HeadQuarters

- Who do you think the heroes are in today's story?
- How would you feel if an angel came and spoke to you? Show me how your face would look if that happened.
- How did the shepherds find baby Jesus?
- Who did the shepherds tell about Jesus' birth?

God loved the shepherds and wanted them to know about Jesus. God wants everyone to know about Jesus. Even though you're young, you can tell people about Jesus just as the shepherds did.

BIBLE REVIEW FIND AND TELL!

Form two groups—shepherds and townspeople. **We are going to play hide and go seek, but in a little different way. Half of us will be shepherds** (point to shepherd group), **and we're going to seek. Half of us will be townspeople** (point to townspeople group), **and we're going to hide. When I count to three, shepherds, cover your eyes and townspeople, go hide. One . . . two . . . three.**

Allow a few moments for the townspeople to find hiding places. Then lead the shepherds in looking for the townspeople, pretending you're traveling in the country, saying things like, "Look, I see someone under that tree. Do you think she would like to hear about Jesus?" Each time you find someone, lead the shepherds in saying, "Jesus is born!"

Continue until you've found all the townspeople, then switch roles and repeat.

The shepherds told everyone they saw about Jesus. You can talk to people you meet every day about Jesus too.

BIBLE MEMORY

Using the Bible Memory activity poster, review the Bible Memory with the children. Draw children's attention to the illustration of the mouth and discuss the different conversations children are having. Ask which conversation shows the wrong way to talk to someone and how that way doesn't show Jesus' love. Invite children to tell you actions they can do to show love or tell about Jesus, giving them opportunities to put stickers on the poster. Then use the Bible Memory Actions found on the CD to review the verse with the children.

After you review the verse, talk with the children about how the verse relates to today's Bible story. **The shepherds in our Bible story had a special message to share. They couldn't wait to tell others about Jesus. We can learn from the shepherds and from our Bible Memory that God wants everyone to know about Jesus, and we can help tell others!**

TEACHING TIPS

If you have stuffed lambs or sheep, place them around the blankets to add to the story atmosphere.

Some children may be familiar with this story. Take time to hear their explanations before going on with the story.

MATERIALS

(optional: *Teaching Resources CD* Track 2 and CD "Shepherds Tell About Jesus" Bible story music activity printable file)

TEACHING TIP

Active children will enjoy reviewing this Bible story as a music activity. Lyrics and suggested actions are included on the resources CD Session 2 "Shepherds Tell About Jesus" printable file.

MATERIALS

Teaching Resources Sheet 7 and CD All Sessions Bible Memory Action (*NIV* or *KJV*) printable file, mini stickers

TEACHING TIPS

Are you remembering to add stickers to the Bible Memory activity poster? (See Session 1, Step 2.) The more kids see you adding stickers, the more good choices you will see.

After the children have learned portions of the Bible Memory, play the Right on Target game found on the resources CD.

LIFE FOCUS: Heroes take ACTION!

MATERIALS

Hero Handbook pp. 5 and 6 and stickers

MATERIALS

none

COOPER SKIT OPTION

Does Cooper really think he can tell the whole world about Jesus? Find out as kids watch today's skit. You can find the audio skit and printable file on *Cooper Skits CD*.

STEP 3 — Use one or more of these activities to help children *identify ways they can tell others about Jesus.*

QUICKSTEP: WHO WILL I TELL?

Remind children that God wants everyone to hear the good news about Jesus. On page 6 in their handbooks, help children identify the people in the pictures and match the number stickers to the people they can tell about Jesus. (Answers: 1. waitress; 2. playmate; 3. teacher; 4. cashier; 5. neighbor.)

If time allows, have the children review the Bible story using the picture of the shepherds on page 5. As you discuss the questions, help the children count the sheep and draw lines to connect shepherds with listeners in the crowd. Remind children that they can be heroes and tell people about Jesus just as the shepherds did.

OPTION 1: WE CAN GO!

Remind children that God wants everyone to hear the good news about Jesus. Ask:
- **What are some ways you can be a hero and tell others about Jesus?**
- **Who can you tell?**
- **Where will you find those people?**

Let's learn a song to help us think of all the places we could tell people about Jesus.

Teach children this simple action song to the tune of "The Farmer in the Dell."

The shepherds went to tell. *(run in place)*
The shepherds went to tell.
God's Son is born! God's Son is born! *(cup hands to mouth)*
The shepherds went to tell. *(run in place)*

They told all over town. *(point all around the room)*
They told all over town.
They told the old, they told the young. *(pretend to stroke beard for "old;" rock baby for "young")*
They told all over town. *(point all around the room)*

We can go and tell. *(point to self and nod)*
We can go and tell.
God's Son is born! God's Son is born! *(cup hands to mouth)*
We can go and tell. *(point to self and nod)*

We can tell at ____. *(let children name places and suggest motions)*
We can tell at ____.
We'll tell the world: God's Son is born! *(cup hands to mouth)*
We can go and tell! *(point to self and nod)*

OPTION 2: GOT TO TELL SOMEBODY!

Before class, print the "Got to Tell Somebody" cup covers from the resources CD. You'll need two covers per child. (Older children may be interested in gluing covers to both of their cups, while younger children will probably be satisfied with just one.) Precut the cup covers for younger children or if you think you'll be running short on time. Poke a small hole in the bottom center of each cup.

Set out the supplies. Help children color the cup covers, then glue the covers onto the cups. Help the children thread yarn or string through the ends of each of their cups. Tie a knot on the inside of each cup to hold the cups in place on the string. To keep the knots from slipping through the cup, tie a large paper clip to each end of the string. Pair children up and show them how to use one set of cups like telephones by putting the cups to their ears to hear and then to their mouths to speak. Let them practice using their phones to tell each other the good news that Jesus is born!

Talk with the children about how the shepherds might have passed the news to their friends and family. Point out that the shepherds didn't have phones or cars, so they had to walk everywhere to tell the news. **Our heroes in today's Bible story had an important job! Even though the shepherds probably had to travel far, they couldn't wait to tell everyone the good news about Jesus. Who can you tell about Jesus?**

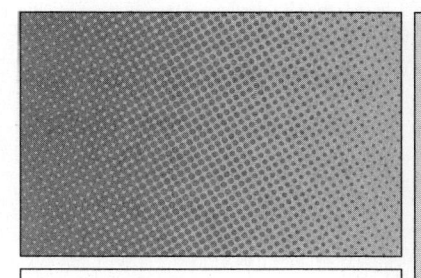

MATERIALS

12-oz plastic cups, *Teaching Resources CD* Session 2 "Got to Tell Somebody!" printable file, yarn or string, scissors, washable markers or crayons, glue, small paper clips

TEACHING TIP

This is a great opportunity to help children connect baby Jesus with the Lord who died for them. Use this time to explain that God loved us so much, He sent Jesus to be born as a baby, then grow up to die on the cross and rise again. Answer any questions children have and remind them that they can share the good news about Jesus' resurrection too.

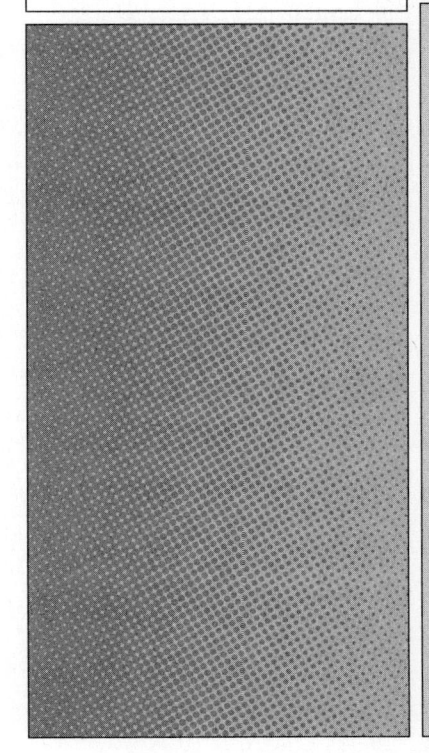

LIFE FOCUS: Heroes take ACTION!

MATERIALS

Teaching Resources CD Session 2 shepherds' announcement printable file, washable markers or crayons, *Teaching Resources CD* Track 1 and CD All Sessions "Stand Up!" printable file, CD player

TEACHING TIPS

Consider using digital photos of the children and have children add yarn or straw to the manger.

Need something to get the kids settled down before they go home or to closing assembly? Watching *The Story of Christmas* from the *Happy Day® 5-Book Set* or *Happy Day® Digital Book Bundle* will not only calm them down but will reinforce the story of Jesus' birth—a story that never gets too old to tell.

STEP 4 — Use this activity to help each child *choose a way to be a hero who tells about Jesus.*

QUICK STEP: ANNOUNCING...JESUS!

Before class, print the two pages of the shepherds' announcement from the resources CD, *back-to-back,* one per child. Set out markers or crayons and let children color the announcements and draw a picture of themselves as shepherds. Younger children may need help filling in their facial features.

Direct children's attention to the shepherds' announcement. As children work, talk about baby announcements. Point out that their parents probably sent out announcements to let people know a special baby had arrived. The announcement they will be making is for a very special baby—Jesus! Help each child identify a specific person to receive the announcement. Write that person's name on the back. Congratulate children for their good work in sharing the news about Jesus!

Close the session by singing "Stand Up!" The song and lyrics can be found on the resources CD.

From the *PreSchool Teaching Resources CD* Session 2 printable file

• Add your own news or leave as is and print copies of the **Hero HeadQuarters Family Page**. It lets parents know what their kids are learning and gives an overview of the Bible story, as well as suggests ways they can encourage their children to be heroes, telling someone about Jesus!

• Print copies of **Shepherds Tell About Jesus Puzzle** onto card stock. Kids will love making puzzles to take home. Have a supply of envelopes handy for them to put their puzzle pieces in.

• Print copies of **Shepherds Tell About Jesus Coloring Page** for kids to take home and color with their friends and families.

For more fun, have your kids visit these sites (or use the leader's guides):

• *Power Projects*—Choose from a variety of creative and purposeful projects and activities that will help kids remember to be heroes who take action for God!

• *Super Snacks*—Kids will love making and eating these tasty snacks that reinforce the Bible story!

• *Action Games*—Give kids time to move, play, work on hero skills, and relax. All the super fun activities connect to the Bible hero story and Bible focus.

SESSION 3

Heroes step out on FAITH!

BIBLE BACKGROUND

A centurion was a Roman officer in command of a hundred men. When a crowd gathered, his job was to guide his men to keep peace and guard against armed rebellion or mob violence. He understood giving orders and having them obeyed.

When the centurion's servant became so seriously ill that he was suffering, the centurion came to Jesus for help. Jesus agreed to go and heal the servant, but the centurion told Jesus that it was not necessary for Him to come to his house. Jesus could just order the disease to go, and it would go whether or not He was there to watch.

Jesus praised the centurion's faith before the crowd of people. The people of Israel brought the sick to Jesus in great numbers. But none had shown faith enough to believe Jesus could heal anyone without Jesus even seeing him! Jesus told the centurion that He indeed could do what the centurion requested. And He did! The servant was healed at that very time.

What was so heroic about the centurion? In humility, he stepped out on faith, believing in Jesus' power. What an example for us to help us remember that heroes always go to Jesus in faith.

BIBLE STORY
An army officer goes to Jesus, and Jesus heals his servant (Matthew 8:5-10, 13).

BIBLE MEMORY
1 Timothy 4:12

Step 1 Use one or more of these activities to help children *explore what it means to give and follow directions.*	**Step 2** Use this interactive story to help children *tell what the army officer did to show he believed in Jesus.*	**Step 3** Use one or more of these activities to help children *identify ways they can show they believe in Jesus.*	**Step 4** Use this activity to help each child *choose a way to be a hero who shows trust in Jesus.*
QUICK Step: Partner Snack **Materials:** snack, napkins, wet wipes	**Bible Story: Materials:** Bible, *Teaching Resources* Sheet 3	**QUICK Step:** Sing It—Believe It! **Materials:** construction paper, scissors, tape, *Teaching Resources CD*, CD player	**QUICK Step:** Here's How I Show It! **Materials:** *Teaching Resources CD*, CD player
Option 1: Pretend Play **Materials:** uniform dress-up items, full-length mirror	**Bible Review: Materials:** *Hero Handbook* and stickers	**Option 1:** Cozy Corner **Materials:** pillows, children's Bibles, Bible story picture books	**Option 2:** Time to Trust **Materials:** *Hero Handbook* and stickers, scissors, paper fasteners, hole punch
Option 2: Stuff, Fold, Staple, Shake **Materials:** paper plates, stapler, index cards, washable markers, bowl or dish tub, dried beans or rice	**Bible Memory: Materials:** *Teaching Resources* Sheet 7 and CD, mini stickers		

PreSchool Teacher 23

LIFE FOCUS:

Heroes step out on FAITH!

MATERIALS

snack, napkins, wet wipes

MATERIALS

uniform dress-up items, full-length mirror

TEACHING TIP

Make sure you have enough hats, jackets, etc., for each child to dress up in some type of uniform. Ask your congregation for assistance in obtaining these items or check out your secondhand stores.

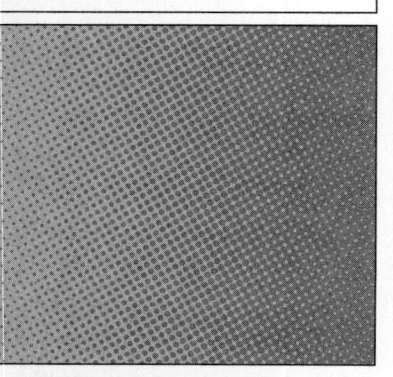

STEP 1 — Use one or more of these activities to help children *explore* what it means to *give and follow directions.*

QUICKSTEP: PARTNER SNACK

Have children clean their hands. Form pairs. Give each pair two napkins. Set out the snack supplies.

Help children take turns giving and following directions as they prepare their partners' snacks. For example, one partner might say, "I want two crackers on this side of my napkin and three on that side," "Please put all my crackers under my napkin," or "I'd like a stack of five crackers."

After both partners have had a turn to give and follow directions, let the children enjoy the snack. As they eat, explain that today's Bible hero story is about an army officer who gave directions to his soldiers, but he followed directions from Jesus.

ESPECIALLY FOR 3s!

Giving each other commands will be difficult for younger children. As the teacher, give simple commands for them to follow.

OPTION 1: PRETEND PLAY

Before class, prepare an area for dress-up play. Be sure to include a mirror so that children can see themselves when they put on the uniform dress-ups.

Direct children to the dress-up area. Show them the uniform clothing and help them choose what they'll wear to dress up. Talk to them about the jobs represented by the different uniforms. Point out that many people in uniform give other people directions as part of their jobs. Encourage children to practice giving and following directions with each other as part of their pretend play.

As children play, ask:
- **How do these people give directions?**
- **Why is it important to learn to follow directions?**
- **Tell about a time when you had to follow directions at home or school.**

Police and firefighters give directions that help keep people safe. Parents and teachers also give directions for us to follow. Our hero in today's Bible story is an army officer. He was used to giving directions to his soldiers, but today we'll hear what happened when Jesus gave *him* some directions.

OPTION 2: STUFF, FOLD, STAPLE, SHAKE

Before class, make a sample of the shaker to show to the kids. Set up two tables. On one table, put three index cards labeled 1, 2, and 3. On the other table put the remaining supplies in three piles: 1) paper plates and markers, 2) stapler, and 3) bowl of dried beans or rice. As part of this activity, children will help determine the steps needed to make shakers.

We have a special project to do today (show shaker)**, but we're missing the directions. Hmm. There are three things we need to do.** Point to the three numbered index cards. **These are the supplies we'll need. Let's see if we can figure out what we should do first, second, and third to make a musical instrument out of these supplies.**

Help children as needed to put the supplies in order. Talk about the directions they'll need to follow: First, color the plates. Second, add a handful of beans. Third, staple the plates together so the beans don't fall out. Help children think about what would happen if they did the steps out of order, or left out one or more steps.

Following directions is important! Directions keep us safe and help us do the things we want or need to do. Our hero in today's Bible story is an army officer who was in charge of giving directions to soldiers. Let's find out what directions he received from Jesus.

MATERIALS

paper plates, stapler, index cards, washable markers, bowl or dish tub, dried beans or rice (optional: crepe streamers)

TEACHING TIP

Plain, non-waxy paper plates work best for coloring.

TEACHING TIP

Preschoolers' ability to follow directions may vary, depending on the age of your students. Threes can follow one- and some two-step directions. Fours and fives should be able to follow two- or three-step directions independently. For this project, three steps are required. Support children as needed to determine the order of the steps, then complete the project. Streamers are an optional touch you can add at the end.

LIFE FOCUS: Heroes step out on FAITH!

MATERIALS

Bible, *Teaching Resources* Sheet 3 (optional: *Happy Day® 5-Book Set* or *Happy Day® Digital Book Bundle*)

TEACHING TIPS

Have a helper to assist children with the actions as you tell the story.

Introduce the story of the centurion using *New Testament Faith Heroes* from the *Happy Day® 5-Book Set* or *Happy Day® Digital Book Bundle*. This will calm down the children to be ready to participate in the Bible story.

STEP 2 Use this interactive story to help children *tell what the army officer did to show he believed in Jesus.*

BIBLE STORY: AN ARMY OFFICER GOES TO JESUS, AND JESUS HEALS HIS SERVANT

Open the Bible to Matthew 8 and place it on your lap. Show children Sheet 3. Point to the army officer and talk about his uniform. If the children tried on uniforms in Step 1, have them compare what they tried on to the army officer's uniform. **I need you to help me with our Bible story today. Each time you hear me say the words *army officer*, salute like this.** Demonstrate a simple salute by putting your hand to your forehead and standing at attention. Have children practice saluting once or twice.

When you hear the word *sick*, or *sickness*, rub your stomach like this. Demonstrate and have children practice with you.

When you hear the word *servant* get on your knees. Demonstrate and have children practice with you.

When you hear the word *faith*, put your hands together as if you are praying. *Faith* means believing in Jesus, and we're going to hear about an amazing thing Jesus did for someone who believed in Him. Demonstrate praying hands and have children practice with you.

Read the Bible story to the children. Pause after the **boldface** words for children to do the motions they have practiced.

OK, now we are ready for the story. This story is about an **army officer**. He was an important **army officer** who gave directions to a lot of men. Do you remember the important man in another story we heard at VBS? The story about the **servant** girl who helped her master? Well, this **army officer** had a **servant** too. His **servant** was **sick**. Jesus was healing many people and this **army officer** heard about Jesus. The **army officer** had great **faith**. He believed in Jesus! The **army officer** asked Jesus if He would help his **servant**. What do you think Jesus' answer was to the **army officer**?

Jesus said He would go see the **servant** and heal him of his **sickness**. But the **army officer** knew Jesus was very busy. There were so many people who needed Jesus! The **army officer** trusted Jesus so much, he believed that Jesus could help his **servant** without even seeing him! The **army officer** believed that Jesus could just tell the **sickness** to go away and the **sickness** would go away, and the **servant** would be healed. What do you think? Could Jesus heal the **servant** without even going to see the **servant**? Of course He could! Jesus can do anything!

Jesus said the **army officer** had great **faith** because he believed that if Jesus gave directions to the **sickness,** it would go away. And guess what? Jesus did heal the **servant**, right on the spot—without even going to see the **servant**—just as the **army officer** believed Jesus would.

The army officer is our Bible hero for today because he showed his faith by trusting Jesus to heal his servant. We can show our faith by singing, praying, telling others about Jesus, or showing Jesus' love by our kind and loving actions.

BIBLE REVIEW

The army officer was used to giving directions, but it was Jesus who gave the directions in our Bible story. Jesus directed the sickness to stop, and it stopped! Now it's your turn to give and follow directions to help us review our story.

Choose three older children to be leaders. Help the rest of the children form three groups. Have one group do the motions for "army officer," the second group do "servant," and the third group do "faith." Assign a leader to each group. Remind children to watch their leaders for directions.

Read the story again and let children act out the motions in their groups. Remind them to only do the actions they see their leaders do.

Have children look at the Bible story picture on page 7 of their handbooks. Let children put the stickers where they belong. If desired, provide sand for them to glue onto the road. Discuss the questions and encourage children to share ways they can trust in Jesus as the army officer did.

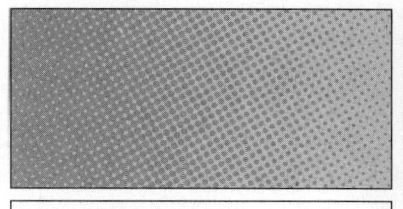

MATERIALS

Hero Handbook p. 7 and stickers (optional: *Teaching Resources CD* Session 3 "Just Say the Word" printable file)

TEACHING TIP

Younger children will enjoy singing "Just Say the Word" to the tune of "She'll Be Coming 'Round the Mountain" to review today's story.

BIBLE MEMORY

Using the Bible Memory activity poster, review the Bible Memory with the children. Draw children's attention to the illustration of the Bible and discuss the situations shown. Assure children that they can talk to Jesus anytime and they can trust Him to take care of them just as He took care of the army officer's servant. Remind them that even children can trust and believe in Jesus. Invite children to tell you actions they can do to show faith in Jesus, giving them opportunities to put stickers on the poster. Then use the Bible Memory Actions or the game found on the resources CD to review the verse with the children.

After you review the verse, talk with the children about how the verse relates to today's Bible story. **Today we learned about an army officer who had a sick servant. The army officer went to see Jesus because he believed Jesus could heal his servant. He had great faith. Our Bible Memory tells us that even though you're young, you can have great faith and believe in Jesus just as the army officer did.**

MATERIALS

Teaching Resources Sheet 7 and CD All Sessions Bible Memory Actions *(NIV* or *KJV)* printable file, mini stickers

TEACHING TIP

Remember to add stickers to the Bible Memory activity poster. (See Session 1, Step 2.) The more kids see you adding stickers, the more good choices you will see.

After the children have learned portions of the Bible Memory, play the Right on Target game found on the resources CD.

PreSchool Teacher 27

LIFE FOCUS:

Heroes step out on FAITH!

MATERIALS

construction paper, scissors, tape, *Teaching Resources CD* Track 1 and CD All Sessions "Stand Up!" printable file, CD player

MATERIALS

pillows, children's Bibles, Bible story picture books

COOPER SKIT OPTION

Kids will enjoy watching Cooper as he discovers that believing doesn't always require seeing. You can find the audio skit and printable file on *Cooper Skits CD*.

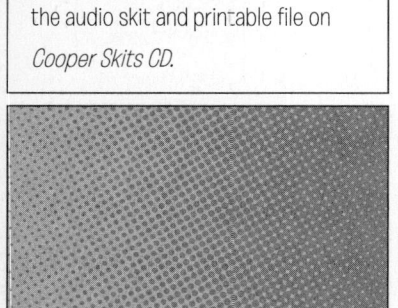

STEP 3 Use one or more of these activities to help children *identify ways they can show they believe in Jesus.*

QUICKSTEP: SING IT! BELIEVE IT!

Before class, cut out large footprints from the construction paper, one per child, plus a few extra. Mark one of the footprints with a star. Tape the footprints to the floor around the room. Have ready situations that children will tell a way they can trust in Jesus (e.g., a bad storm is coming; you are afraid to sleep in the dark; your grandmother is very sick; you are moving to a new town).

Singing and telling are ways we can show we believe in Jesus. We can use words to show what's in our hearts. So let's march and sing "Stand Up!" When I stop the music, I will give a situation to the child who is standing on the star. I want him to tell us how he will trust in Jesus in that situation.

Have children sing "Stand Up!" as they march around the room on the footprints. Pause the CD and give a situation to the child who is standing on the star. If he isn't able to tell a way he will trust in Jesus, let him ask a friend to help him. This is a good time to remind children that Jesus gives us friends when we need help.

Especially for 3s!

Mark several footprints with a star. Then when children land on the stars, have those children shout, "Jesus, I believe in You," instead of having them tell how they can trust Jesus in a situation.

OPTION 1: COZY CORNER

Set up a cozy corner with children's Bibles, Bible storybooks, and pillows. If possible, provide at least one book for every two children. Invite children to look at books with teachers, friends, or on their own.

Reading Bible stories is a great way to learn more about Jesus and show we believe in Him. We can tell our friends and family about the great things Jesus has done and about how much He loves each one of us.

Invite children to tell you about their favorite Bible stories. If possible, find the stories in the books and look at the pictures together.

- **Do you like someone to read the Bible to you? Do you like looking at the pictures?**
- **What Bible stories do you know? Which one is your favorite?**
- **Do you know someone who likes to read the Bible?**

You can read Bible stories at home too. Ask an older brother or sister or a grownup to help you!

OPTION 2: TIME TO TRUST

MATERIALS

Hero Handbook and stickers, scissors, paper fasteners, hole punch

Let children decorate their clocks using the stickers from the handbook insert. Then help children cut out the minute and hour hands and attach them to the clock using the paper fasteners. Show children how to move the hands, saying the times of the day with them (eleven o'clock at night, nine o'clock in the morning, etc.). As they move the hands, talk with them about the activities you do at various times of the day (morning, mealtimes, afternoon, bedtime). As you do each time, ask children to share what they do during the same time. Show children what time of the day you pray and invite them to point to the time they pray or read Bible stories.

- **When is your favorite time to pray? Mealtimes? Bedtime?**
- **Where is your favorite place to pray?**

Remind children that praying is a way to show trust in Jesus. Discuss things children might pray about or thank God for. Tell children that any time is a good time to pray, including right now at VBS! Take time to pray with the children.

Especially for 3s!

Some children may not have cutting skills. Cut out their clock hands before class time to preserve the Bible story picture on page 7.

SESSION 3

PreSchool Teacher 29

LIFE FOCUS:

Heroes step out on **FAITH!**

MATERIALS

Teaching Resources CD Track 1, CD player

From the PreSchool *Teaching Resources CD* Session 3 printable file, send home with each child
- Hero HeadQuarters Family Page—add your own news or leave as is and print copies.
- An Army Officer Goes to Jesus Puzzle—printed on card stock.
- An Army Officer Goes to Jesus Coloring Page

Have kids visit these sites (or use the leader's guides):
- Power Projects—Choose from a variety of creative and purposeful projects and activities.
- Super Snacks—Kids will make and eat these tasty snacks that reinforce the Bible story!
- Action Games—Give kids time to move, play, work on hero skills, and relax.

STEP 4
Use this activity to help each child *choose a way to be a hero who shows trust in Jesus.*

QUICKSTEP: HERE'S HOW I SHOW IT!

Invite each child to choose a way to show trust in Jesus: singing about Him, telling someone about Him (or sharing a favorite Bible story), or praying. Have children gather in groups according to which way they've chosen. Have the singing group stand in front while the other two groups sit down. Say:

Jesus loves me and Jesus loves you.

You can sing this great message to friends—old and new. *(have children link arms and sway)*

If you can sing . . . sing anything!

Ready, set, sing!

Lead singers in singing "Jesus Loves Me" and then have them sit down. Invite the tellers to stand. Give them a moment to think of who they'll tell or what Bible story they'd like to share. Say:

You can show trust by telling the news.

You can tell anyone—who will you choose? *(have several children share)*

If you can tell . . . get ready to yell:

Jesus, I believe! Jesus, I believe!

Have the tellers shout, "Jesus, I believe!" Invite the rest of the children to join you. Signal to end shouting. Have the tellers sit down. Invite the prayers to stand. Encourage them to think of a specific time when they'll pray. Say:

If you can pray, now it's your turn to play!

If you'll pray before bed, now tap your head.

If you'll pray when you eat, please stomp your feet.

Hip, hip, hooray—we can all pray!

Invite all the children to stand and join you in three cheers.

Then ask children for ideas of how they will be heroes and trust Jesus just as the army officer did in today's story.

Close in prayer: **Dear God, thank You for loving us and taking care of us. Thank You that we can pray to You anytime. Help us this week to pray and sing and share the good news about Jesus. We believe in Him! Amen.** Close the session with everyone singing "Stand Up!"

ESPECIALLY FOR 3s!
Do all activities together as one large group.

SESSION 4

Heroes SAVE THE DAY!

BIBLE BACKGROUND

Nearing the time of the Jewish Passover, Jesus suggested that He and His disciples go on a retreat (Mark 6:30, 31) because much had been happening in the disciples' and Jesus' ministries. So Jesus and His disciples crossed over the Sea of Galilee. When they went up on a mountainside and sat down, Jesus saw people coming to meet them. They wanted to see this man who performed miracles on the sick!

Jesus would not disappoint the people who had traveled so far. They needed Him too. Jesus, knowing what He was going to do next, tested the disciples by telling them to go find some food.

Imagine their surprise! Where could they find that much food? If they found it, how could they afford to buy it? Andrew found a boy who had brought five loaves of bread and two fish with him, but how far could that go? Jesus knew!

Jesus had the people sit down, and then He gave thanks to His Heavenly Father who truly provided. Everyone ate as much bread and fish as they wanted. All because a boy shared his food, the day was saved and thousands of people were well fed.

What can you do today that would "save" someone's day? Let's look for ways to give what we have and let Jesus use it for His heroic purposes.

BIBLE STORY
A boy shares his food, and Jesus feeds more than 5,000 people (John 6:1-13).

BIBLE MEMORY
1 Timothy 4:12

Step 1	Step 2	Step 3	Step 4
Use one or more of these activities to help children *explore big numbers*.	Use this interactive story to help children *tell what a boy did to help others*.	Use one or more of these activities to help children *identify ways they can help others*.	Use this activity to help each child *choose a way to be a hero who helps others*.
QUICK Step: Heroes Save the Day — **Materials:** *Hero Handbook*, crayons	**Bible Story:** — **Materials:** Bible, *Teaching Resources CD*, lunch bag, canvas bag, 2 paper fish, 5 bread rolls, 12 baskets	**QUICK Step:** Who Can Help? — **Materials:** none	**QUICK Step:** Helping Hands — **Materials:** *Hero Handbook* and stickers, *Teaching Resources CD*, CD player, crayons
Option 1: Guess How Many? — **Materials:** large clear jar, goldfish crackers, measuring cup, napkins, cups of water, wet wipes, *Teaching Resources* Sheet 4	**Bible Review:** — **Materials:** *Teaching Resources CD*, brown construction paper, scissors	**Option 1:** Flashy Fish — **Materials:** *Teaching Resources CD*, poster board, washable markers or watercolor paints, glue, blunt-tip scissors	
Option 2: Parachute of Plenty — **Materials:** play parachute, loaf of bread	**Bible Memory:** — **Materials:** *Teaching Resources* Sheet 7 and CD, mini stickers	**Option 2:** Hide and Find Helpers — **Materials:** helping items (see p. 37), bright colored ribbon	

PreSchool Teacher 31

LIFE FOCUS:
Heroes SAVE THE DAY!

MATERIALS

Hero Handbook p. 9, crayons

MATERIALS

large clear jar or bowl, goldfish crackers, 1 cup measuring cup, napkins, cups of water, wet wipes, Teaching Resources Sheet 4

(optional: Happy Day® 5-Book Set or Happy Day® Digital Book Bundle)

TEACHING TIPS

Be sensitive to food allergies when providing snacks for preschoolers. If a child has a dairy allergy, use pretzel goldfish. If a child has wheat or gluten allergies, gluten-free pretzels are available in other shapes.

While kids are in the mode of counting, they will enjoy counting along with the reader while watching Five Small Loaves and Two Small Fish from the Happy Day® 5-Book Set or Happy Day® Digital Book Bundle.

STEP 1 — Use one or more of these activities to help children *explore big numbers*.

QUICKSTEP: HEROES SAVE THE DAY!

Show children the handbook page with the Bible story picture. Help the children count the loaves and circle the missing fish in the picture. Ask the children if they can count the people in the crowd. Explain that there were so many people, they couldn't all fit in the picture!

Our Bible story hero for today is a boy who probably wasn't much older than you. Let's find out who he was and how he helped Jesus.

OPTION 1: GUESS HOW MANY?

Before class, transfer a box or bag of fish crackers into a clear jar or bowl. Fill a one cup measuring cup and count how many fish fit inside. Use this number to estimate how many fish are in the bowl. It doesn't have to be exact.

Have children wash their hands and then sit in a circle around the jar of fish crackers.

I wonder how many fish crackers are in this big jar. What are your guesses? I wonder if we could count that high!

Count out loud with children for one or two of their guesses, then put crackers on each child's napkin, giving each child an equal amount. Invite children to count their crackers, then count together to see if you can count everyone's crackers. Be sure to count quickly, because the crackers will disappear!

As children enjoy the crackers, invite them to count other things in the classroom. How many children are at VBS today? How many blocks are in the room? How many crayons? How many empty chairs are there?

Show children the Bible story poster. **It sure would take a lot of food to feed all of these people! Where have you been when you were in a crowd of people? Were you at a basketball game? Were you at church? Were you at the airport? If everyone got hungry at the same time and there was no food around, what do you think the people would do?** (If no one mentions it, say that people would start asking others for something to eat.)

Let children respond, then continue: **Well, that was exactly what happened in our Bible story. Let's find out who today's Bible story hero is and how he helped Jesus.**

OPTION 2: PARACHUTE OF PLENTY

MATERIALS

play parachute, loaf of bread

TEACHING TIP

If a play parachute isn't available to you, use a bedsheet. Or purchase a parachute online at a school supply store, such as S&S Worldwide at www.ssww.com.

Consider what would work best in your classroom or outdoor environment as you plan this activity to help children explore big numbers in a fun, hands-on way. You could have children tear many pieces from a large loaf of bread as described (best for outside), or collect small soft toys from around your classroom. If you use toys, make sure they are soft so they won't hurt if they fly off the parachute (no blocks, cars, etc.). If you use bread, use this opportunity to share with the birds! Remind children that God loves them much more than He loves the birds and flowers.

Show children the bread. Break it into large pieces and give a piece to each child. Have children break their pieces into smaller pieces and place them in the center of the parachute or sheet.

- **How many pieces (toys) do you think we have?**
- **How many people do you think our bread would feed?**
- **What can we do with this bread we have broken up?**

Lead children in playing with the parachute. Have them try the following motions: sitting around (not on) the edge of the parachute, sitting on the edge of the parachute, walking around in a circle while holding onto the parachute, shaking the parachute (watch out for flying bread or toys), lifting the parachute up high and then lowering it at different speeds.

How else can we use this parachute? (Allow responses.) **Let's count one thousand, two thousand, three thousand, four thousand, five thousand. When we say five thousand, let's lift the parachute high and all run under it. Ready? One thousand, two thousand, three thousand, four thousand, five thousand!**

Gather children under the parachute. **Being under this parachute is like being in God's loving care. God is always all around us. He'll always take care of us. Let's find out about today's Bible hero and how Jesus used him to help the people in a crowd.**

PreSchool Teacher 33

SESSION 4

LIFE FOCUS: Heroes SAVE THE DAY!

MATERIALS

Bible, *Teaching Resources CD* Session 4 Boy puppet printable file, lunch bag, canvas bag, 2 paper fish, 5 bread rolls, 12 baskets

BEFORE CLASS

Print out the boy puppet from the resources CD and assemble according to instructions on the printable file. Place the two fish and five loaves of bread in the canvas bag. Set the 12 baskets out of sight until the end of the story.

TEACHING TIPS

If you don't have woven baskets, use small reusable plastic containers.

A printable fish pattern is provided on the resources CD, Session 4.

STEP 2 — Use this interactive story to help children *tell what a boy did to help others.*

BIBLE STORY: A BOY SHARES HIS FOOD, AND JESUS FEEDS MORE THAN 5,000 PEOPLE

Open the Bible to John 6 and place it on your lap. **Have you ever been in a big, enormous group of people?** Let children share. **I have a friend who has a story to tell about how Jesus used him to help others. Let me have him come and share his story with you.** Bring out the puppet to tell the story.

One day I was hiking on a mountainside when I saw a *big* group of people. More and more people kept coming and the crowd got bigger and bigger and bigger. *(Make arms get bigger and bigger.)* I wondered how many people were there, but there were too many to count!

I looked all around *(look with your hands over your eyes)* to find out what was happening. Then I saw that all those people were listening to a man. Who was He? I listened closely to hear what He was saying. *(Put your hand in back of your ear.)*

All of those people were listening to a kind teacher whose name was Jesus. Have you heard of Jesus? What can you tell me about Him? *(Let children share.)*

No wonder so many people wanted to hear Jesus! He can heal people who are sick, and He sometimes performs miracles. Miracles are amazing! The people didn't want to miss any miracles or anything that Jesus was saying. They listened to Jesus all day long.

But that was longer than they expected. After a while they began to get hungry. What does your tummy sound like when you're hungry? How does it feel?

It was a good thing my mommy had made me a picnic lunch! I was SO hungry, and I was just getting ready to open my lunch. Fish and bread . . . yum-yum! *(Take one of the fish and pretend you're about to feed it to the puppet.)*

I was about to eat my lunch when one of Jesus' friends stopped me. He asked what I had in my lunch. I showed him the two little fish and five small loaves of bread. *(Hold up fish and bread.)* So Jesus' friend took me to Jesus.

I knew my little lunch wasn't enough to feed that huge, enormous, gigantic *(make arms get bigger and bigger)* crowd, but I gave it to Jesus anyway. I had no idea what He was going to do with it.

Jesus asked the people to sit. He prayed and thanked God for the food. Then Jesus' friends began to pass the food around to all of those people. Would there be enough for everyone? Would there be any left for me?

Yes! I don't know how Jesus did it, but everyone had enough to eat. No one was hungry anymore *and* there were even 12 baskets of bread left over! *(Bring out the baskets.)* Count them with me: 1-2-3-4-5-6-7-8-9-10-11-12!

And that's my story. Jesus fed more than 5,000 people that day! And I got to help Him by sharing my lunch! I'm sure you are good helpers too.

BIBLE REVIEW

Before class, make copies of the fish pattern from the resources CD. Cut bread loaf shapes from the construction paper.

Let's review our Bible story, then learn a song about the boy who shared his picnic lunch with Jesus.
- **How many fish did the boy have? loaves of bread?**
- **How many people did Jesus feed with the boy's lunch?**
- **How many baskets of bread were left over?**

Teach children the following song to the tune of "Mary Had a Little Lamb." Give each child a fish or bread picture. Have children hold up their fish and bread when you sing those words.

**One little boy had fish and bread,
fish and bread, fish and bread.
One little boy had fish and bread
inside his picnic lunch.**

**Jesus took the fish and bread,
fish and bread, fish and bread.
Jesus gave thanks for fish and bread
and made it a whole bunch!**

BIBLE MEMORY

Using the poster, review the Bible Memory. Draw children's attention to the illustration of the heart and discuss the situations. Ask which situation shows a child not showing love to someone else. Point out that we can show love in everything we do—even something as simple as sharing a lunch like the boy in today's story! Talk with children about their daily activities and help them identify ways they can show Jesus' love. Invite children to tell you which action they can do to show Jesus' love to someone else, giving them opportunities to put stickers on the poster. Then use the Bible Memory Actions found on the resources CD to review the verse with the children.

After you review the verse, talk with the children about how the verse relates to today's Bible story. **Our Bible hero today was a young boy just like you. He was a great example to that great big crowd. He shared his lunch, but he also listened to and trusted Jesus. He helped Jesus feed all those people! You can show Jesus' love by being a helper just as the boy was. Who can you help? Who can you show Jesus' love to?**

MATERIALS

Teaching Resources CD Session 4 fish pattern printable file, brown construction paper, scissors

(optional: *Teaching Resources CD* Track 3 and CD "A Boy Shares His Food" Bible story music activity printable file)

TEACHING TIP

Active children will enjoy reviewing this Bible story as a music activity. Lyrics and suggested actions are included on the resources CD Session 4 "A Boy Shares His Food" printable file.

MATERIALS

Teaching Resources Sheet 7 and CD All Sessions Bible Memory Actions *(NIV* or *KJV)* printable file, mini stickers

TEACHING TIPS

Don't forget to add stickers to the Bible Memory activity poster. (See Session 1, Step 2.) The more kids see you adding stickers, the more good choices you will see.

After the children have learned portions of the Bible Memory, play the Right on Target game found on the resources CD.

LIFE FOCUS:

Heroes SAVE THE DAY!

MATERIALS

none

MATERIALS

Teaching Resources CD Session 4 fish pattern, poster board, washable markers or watercolor paints, glue, blunt-tip scissors

TEACHING TIP

For older children, write one or two words from the Bible Memory on each puzzle piece. Have children repeat the Bible Memory as they put the fish together.

SESSION 4

STEP 3
Use one or more of these activities to help children *identify ways they can help others.*

QUICK STEP: WHO CAN HELP?

Before class, arrange for a simple service project the preschoolers can do for the church. Picking up trash around the church building, washing toys for the nursery, or straightening Bibles and songbooks are just a few ideas.

Today we are going to find some ways we can be heroes by helping others right here in our church building. Can you think of any jobs that we could do?

Invite children to identify ways they can help the church. Introduce the project you've chosen and lead children in completing it. After you've finished, talk about the experience with the children.

• **How did it feel to be a hero?**

• **What are some ways you could be a hero at home? at school? at the grocery store?**

You don't have to be grown up to be a hero and help others. You can be a hero and help others right now, wherever you go!

ESPECIALLY FOR 3s!

If you can find an unused room during VBS, mess it up a bit for the kids to clean. This will keep all the kids contained in one room.

OPTION 1: FLASHY FISH

Before class, cut from poster board one large fish shape for every 4–6 children. Set out the fish shapes and markers or watercolors.

Show children one of the fish shapes. **This fish reminds me of the fish in our Bible story. We're going to work together to color a fish. Then I'll help you cut your fish into a puzzle so you can put it back together. You'll have to work together to get all of the pieces.**

Form groups of 4–6 children and give each group a fish shape to decorate together. As groups finish, help children cut the fish into puzzle pieces. For older fours and fives, you can just draw lines for the children to cut. Three-year-olds will need help cutting. Put children's names on their individual fish pieces to show how they work together to make a whole.

Great job working together! It's great to help each other when we have a big job to do. The next time you see a friend who needs help with something, be a hero and say, "Let me help you!" God is pleased when we are heroes and help one another, just as the boy in our story helped Jesus.

OPTION 2: HIDE AND FIND HELPERS

Help children understand that there are many things they can do that are big ways to help others. Before class, hide the helping items (one per child) around the room at children's eye level. Tie a bright colored ribbon on each of the items you have hidden so children will recognize which items are part of the hunt. Each item they find will give children a clue about a way they can be helpers.

Opportunities to be a hero are all around us every day. Right now, look around our room. See if you can find anything with a colorful ribbon on it. When you find something, bring it back to the group.

Let children look for the items, then gather in a circle. Invite children to share ways they can help others by using each of the items. For example, they could bring a parent a diaper or other supplies for a baby sibling, or use a plate or place mat to help set the table. After you've identified all the items, encourage children to comment on additional ways they can help.

Keep your eyes and ears open. The boy in our Bible story today had no idea he would be a hero and get to help Jesus that day. We never know when a chance to be a hero will come our way either, but we can be ready to help others at any time.

MATERIALS

helping items (e.g., place mat, plastic plate, dustpan, broom, feather duster, disposable diaper, washcloth, box of tissues), bright colored ribbon

COOPER SKIT OPTION

When Cooper goes to a birthday party, he doesn't know he is going to save the day, but he does! You can find the Cooper audio skit and printable file on *Cooper Skits CD*.

PreSchool Teacher 37

LIFE FOCUS: Heroes SAVE THE DAY!

MATERIALS

Hero Handbook pp. 10, 13, and 14 and stickers, crayons, *Teaching Resources CD* Track 1 and CD All Sessions "Stand Up!" printable file, CD player

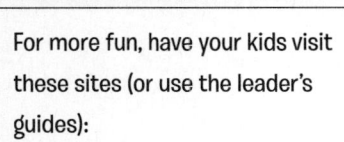

For more fun, have your kids visit these sites (or use the leader's guides):
- **Power Projects**—Choose from a variety of creative and purposeful projects and activities that will help kids remember to be heroes who save the day!
- **Super Snacks**—Kids will love making and eating these tasty snacks that reinforce the Bible story.
- **Action Games**—Give kids time to move, play, work or hero skills, and relax. All the super fun activities connect to the Bible hero story and Bible focus.

STEP 4
Use this activity to help each child *choose a way to be a hero who helps others.*

QUICKSTEP: HELPING HANDS

Show children the handbook page illustrations. Talk about the ways the children in the pictures are being heroes by helping. Invite children to choose two ways they'd like to help. Remind them that they don't have to help in exactly the same way as the child in the picture. Encourage them to tell you what they'll do. Help children trace their hands around the illustrations that represent the ways they've chosen to help.

We sure had fun today, didn't we? We learned about a boy who shared his . . . toys? No? Shared his room with his brother? No? Shared his lunch? Oh yes! Our Bible hero shared his five loaves and two fish, and he helped Jesus feed 5,000 people! What a great miracle that was. What did Jesus do to make that happen? Jesus prayed and thanked God for the food that the boy shared. We can thank God too. Let's thank God now for our fun day learning about Him with our new friends. Pray, **Dear God, thanks for our Bible story about the boy who helped by sharing his lunch. Help us to be heroes and help wherever we go. In Jesus' name, amen.**

Let children add stickers to page 13 of their handbooks. If children can write their own names, have them do this on page 14. Have children cut apart the cards. Talk about each picture. Ask them whom they will be heroes to in each situation and help them write those names on the back of the cards. Remind children to take the cards home and be heroes, doing what is shown on the card.

While children are waiting for their parents or closing assembly time, let them play with the fish puzzles they decorated in Step 3.

Close session by singing "Stand Up!" from the resources CD.

From the *PreSchool Teaching Resources CD* Session 4 printable file
- Add your own news or leave as is and print copies of the **Hero HeadQuarters Family Page.** It lets parents know what their kids are learning and gives an overview of the Bible story, as well as suggests ways they can encourage their children to be heroes, saving the day!
- Print copies of **A Boy Shares His Food Puzzle** onto card stock. Kids will love making puzzles to take home. Have a supply of envelopes handy for them to put their puzzle pieces in.
- Print copies of **A Boy Shares His Food Coloring Page** for kids to take home and color with their friends and families.

SESSION 5

Heroes stand for TRUTH!

BIBLE BACKGROUND

Paul's life seems to have been one crisis after another. In Caesarea, the prophet Agabus brought an ominous warning: if Paul persisted in going on to Jerusalem, he would be seized by the Jews and turned over to the Gentiles. This warning did not deter Paul from going on to Jerusalem (Acts 20:1–21:16). In Jerusalem he was attacked by a mob in the temple, and he might well have been murdered had the Romans not intervened. Paul attempted to make a defense before the temple mob, but his account of his conversion only intensified their rage. As a result, the Romans held him in protective custody until a more formal hearing could be made the next day (Acts 21:17–22:29).

The next morning a group of Jews plotted a conspiracy to kill Paul. More than forty men vowed not to eat or drink until Paul was dead. Hearing this, Paul's nephew acted quickly and told Paul of the plan. Paul sent the young man to report the conspiracy to the Roman commander in charge. From this news, Paul was moved to Caesarea for his protection. Paul had suffered some harrowing experiences, but the Lord had plans that Paul would not only testify in Jerusalem, but also in Rome.

Because Paul's nephew stood for truth, many more people heard about salvation through Jesus Christ. His heroic actions can remind us to stand for truth so others will know Jesus.

BIBLE STORY
A young man shows courage, and Paul lives to serve Jesus (Acts 23:12-24).

BIBLE MEMORY
1 Timothy 4:12

Step 1	Step 2	Step 3	Step 4
Use one or more of these activities to help children *explore what it means to show courage*.	Use this interactive story to help children *tell what happened because Paul's nephew did what was right*.	Use one or more of these activities to help children *identify ways they can stand up and do right for Jesus*.	Use this activity to help each child *choose a way to be a hero who does what is right*.
QUICK Step: Be Brave Bingo **Materials:** *Hero Handbook* p. 12, pennies or other game markers	**Bible Story:** **Materials:** Bible, blocks	**QUICK Step:** Wheel of Life Game **Materials:** *Teaching Resources CD*, pencils, large paper clips, crayons or washable markers	**QUICK Step:** Sit Down, Stand Up Song **Materials:** none
Option 1: Hero Shields **Materials:** poster board, crayons or washable markers, blunt-tip scissors, glue, *Teaching Resources CD*	**Bible Review:** **Materials:** *Hero Handbook* p. 11	**Option 1:** Stand Up Snack **Materials:** pretzel sticks, graham crackers, marshmallows, banana or pineapple chunks, cups of water, plates, wet wipes, napkins	
Option 2: Doctor's Office **Materials:** adhesive bandages, cloth bandages, stuffed animals, play doctor's kit	**Bible Memory:** **Materials:** *Teaching Resources* Sheet 7 and CD, mini stickers	**Option 2:** Stand Up Students **Materials:** large binder clips, *Teaching Resources CD*, crayons or washable markers, scissors, CD player	

PreSchool Teacher 39

SESSION 5

LIFE FOCUS:
Heroes stand for **TRUTH!**

MATERIALS
Hero Handbook p. 12, pennies or other game markers

MATERIALS
poster board, crayons or washable markers, blunt-tip scissors, glue, Teaching Resources CD Session 5 Wheel graphics printable file

---

STEP 1 — Use one or more of these activities to help children *explore* what it means to show courage.

QUICKSTEP: BE BRAVE BINGO

Give each child page 12 from the handbooks, along with nine pennies. Explain to children how to play bingo. **Listen as I read off times you might need to be brave. Put a penny on the picture if that situation has happened to you. If I yell out, "Empty space!" I want you to tell about a time you were brave. When you get three pennies in a row, stand up and shout, "Be Brave!"**

Play several games as time allows. Then say, **Today our Bible story hero is a young man who showed courage. He stood up for what's right, even though it was hard.**

OPTION 1: HERO SHIELDS

Before class, print the shield graphics from the resources CD. You'll need one set of graphics for each child. Using the pattern, also on the CD, cut a shield shape out of poster board for each child.

Set out the supplies. Have children cut out the graphics and glue to the shields. Let children decorate their shields using the markers. As they work, talk about what shields are used for. Explain that heroes may use shields for protection in scary situations.

The Bible says our faith is like a shield. When we believe in God, He'll help us be brave and stand up for what's right. Sometimes it's hard to be brave, but we can do it because God is always with us. Today we'll hear about a Bible hero who was brave. Listen to what happened when he stood up for what was right.

Be sure to put children's names on the back of their shields. Use an extra strip of poster board to staple a band onto the back of each child's shield. Show the children how to slip one hand through the loop to hold onto the shield.

• **What pictures are on your shield? Where else have you seen these pictures?**
• **How can the Bible keep you safe against bad things?**
• **How does the Bible help you with your speech? your thoughts? your heart?**

Do you know that sometimes I pretend to put a shield like this around my heart so that people's words will not hurt me? God tells us to be brave and to know that He is always with us. Do you believe that? I do, and it does make me feel brave.

OPTION 2: DOCTOR'S OFFICE

Set up an area of the room to look like a doctor's office, including an exam table, bandages, and a play doctor's kit. Set a variety of stuffed animals in the doctor's office area to serve as "patients." You could also set up a waiting room with chairs and books for children to look at. Ask these questions as children play in the center.

- **Who has been to a doctor's office? Were you hurt or sick?**
- **Did you have to get a shot?**
- **Did you have to let the doctor look down your throat?**
- **How did you show you were brave?**

Some children may want to make first-aid kits that can be kept in their families' cars. In resealable plastic bags, they can put adhesive bandages, antiseptic wipes, tissues (for wiping tears), and individually wrapped wet wipes. You may want children to decorate their bags with stickers or put the stickers inside their bags. The stickers will be a good distraction to get their minds off their pain.

As children play in the center or make their kits, let them discuss their experiences at the doctor's office or about times they might have fallen and received a bandage for a scrape or cut. Affirm that it can be scary when something happens to your body. Remind children that parents and doctors can help them be brave when they find themselves in those scary situations.

Today we're going to hear about a young man who was brave in a different way. He used his courage to stand up for the truth. Let's find out more about our Bible hero now.

MATERIALS

adhesive bandages, cloth bandages, stuffed animals (don't forget Cooper!), play doctor's kit

(optional: adhesive bandages, antiseptic wipes, tissues, individually wrapped wet wipes, resealable plastic bags, strips of stickers)

TEACHING TIP

Although it may not seem that way to adults, being hurt or sick can be very scary for children. Preschoolers who are still developing their large motor skills frequently fall. Learning to pick themselves up and keep going requires perspective, self-control, and, yes, even bravery! Trips to the doctor's office require similar courage, as they may often involve immunizations at this age. This activity helps children see courage not as an abstract idea, but a feeling they can have in real-life situations.

PreSchool Teacher

SESSION 5

LIFE FOCUS: Heroes stand for TRUTH!

MATERIALS

Bible, blocks (optional: *Happy Day® 5-Book Set* or *Happy Day® Digital Book Bundle*)

TEACHING TIPS

Use *Paul's Great Adventures* from the *Happy Day® 5-Book Set* or *Happy Day® Digital Book Bundle* to introduce children to who Paul was. This will calm down the children to be ready to listen to the Bible story.

Preschoolers love to knock down towers! Let the children have fun with this, then help them get from the block area to the story area so that they will all be settled and ready to listen.

STEP 2 — Use this interactive story to help children *tell what happened because Paul's nephew did what was right.*

BIBLE STORY: A YOUNG MAN SHOWS COURAGE, AND PAUL LIVES TO SERVE JESUS

Form two or more groups of children. Give each group the same number of blocks and ask them to build a tower.

You worked hard on your towers, didn't you? What if someone wanted to crash into your tower and knock it down? How could you protect your tower? *(Let the children come up with ideas.)* **Those are great ideas. I have an idea too. Maybe you could hold hands and surround your tower. Or cover it with a blanket so no one would find it. Today we're going to hear a Bible story about a young man who took action to protect someone he loved. Now you can crash your own towers and come get comfortable for our story.**

(Open the Bible to Acts 23 and place it on your lap.) Have you ever heard any Bible stories about Paul? He was a very brave man who loved God so much. He wanted to tell everyone about Jesus. Who do you tell about Jesus?

Paul was brave; he was a hero because he told others about God's love and about Jesus. But some people didn't want Paul to tell people about Jesus. Can you imagine someone not wanting you to talk about Jesus? Well, these mean people wanted to get rid of Paul.

Do any of you have an uncle? *(Explain to the children the difference between nieces/nephews and aunts/uncles.)* Paul had a nephew who heard these mean people talking about wanting to hurt Paul. What do you think Paul's nephew did? *(Allow for responses.)* He could have stayed in his house to hide from the mean people. He could have run away. But he didn't. He went right away to tell the army commander about those mean people.

Do you know what the army commander did? He used over 400 men to protect Paul and he moved Paul to a place where he would be safe. I wonder how Paul was protected? Do you think they put a blanket over Paul to hide him? Do you think they held hands and surrounded him to protect him? Let's try that to see if that would be a good plan.

(Have the children surround you. If you have a large class, have groups of children form a circle around each adult or teen.) Now let's see if we can move our circle to the other corner of the room. *(Move along with the children as they travel across the room. Once you reach your destination, have the children sit down.)*

Thank you for protecting me. You are so brave! Well, because Paul was protected from those mean people, he was able to tell many other people about Jesus. Paul wrote many letters about Jesus, and we can read those letters today in the Bible. I'm glad Paul's nephew decided to be a hero and be brave. You can be brave and stand up for what's right too.

BIBLE REVIEW

I am going to ask you some questions. Listen carefully to hear if these are real things that happened in our Bible story today. If I say something that happened in our story, stand up. Read the following statements:
- There were mean people who wanted to kill Paul.
- Paul's nephew showed courage by fighting a lion.
- Paul's nephew was brave and he told someone about the plan to hurt Paul.
- Paul got to ride an elephant out of danger.
- Because Paul was saved, a lot more people got to hear about Jesus.

I'm so glad that Paul got out of danger. Do you know that you can share the good news about Jesus' love just as Paul did? **Paul's nephew was part of Paul's family. Let's think about ways we can share Jesus' love with our family and friends too.**

Give each child his copy of page 11 of the handbook. Review the Bible story picture page with the children. Help them answer the questions as they finish coloring the picture and trace the lettters.

ESPECIALLY FOR 3s!

Ask 3s questions that they can answer from the picture: What color did you color the nephew's robe? What is the soldier holding?

BIBLE MEMORY

Using the Bible Memory activity poster, review the Bible Memory with the children. Draw children's attention to the illustration of the thought balloon and discuss the situations shown. Ask which situation shows a child not thinking good thoughts. Then use the Bible Memory Actions found on the resources CD to review the verse with the children.

After you review the verse, talk with the children about how the verse relates to today's Bible story. **Paul's nephew was young, but he was not afraid to speak up and do what was right to protect his uncle.**
- How did Paul's nephew stand for what's right?
- How can we stand for what's right?

One way we can stand for what's right is by thinking good thoughts. I'm sure Paul thought about Jesus all day long! When we're thinking about Jesus and what He wants us to do, we don't have room in our minds to think about doing mean things or hurting people's feelings. Let's keep our hearts and minds on Jesus so we can do what's right! Invite children to tell you which action they can do to show Jesus' love to someone else, giving them opportunities to put stickers on the poster.

MATERIALS

Hero Handbook p. 11
(optional: *Cooper Skits CD*)

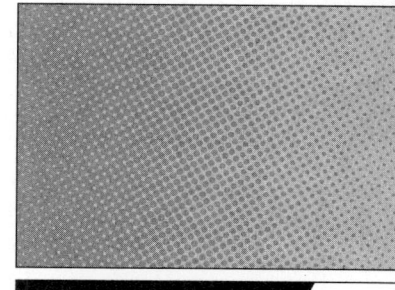

COOPER SKIT OPTION

Let Cooper help the kids review all of the Bible hero stories in today's puppet skit. You can find the audio skit and printable file on *Cooper Skits CD*.

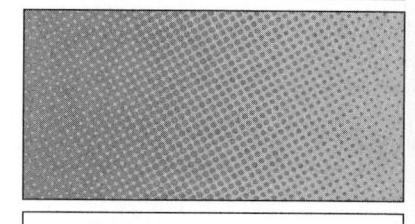

MATERIALS

Teaching Resources Sheet 7 and CD All Sessions Bible Memory Actions *(NIV* or *KJV)* printable file, mini stickers

TEACHING TIP

Have you been adding stickers to the Bible Memory activity poster? Praise kids for all the stickers that are on the poster.

After the children have practiced reciting the Bible Memory, play the Right on Target game found on the resources CD.

SESSION 5

PreSchool Teacher

SESSION 5

LIFE FOCUS: Heroes stand for TRUTH!

MATERIALS

Teaching Resources CD Session 5 Wheel of Life, sharpened pencils, large paper clips, crayons or washable markers

TEACHING TIP

Print the game on card stock to make it more durable. Kids will enjoy taking the game home and playing it with their friends.

MATERIALS

pretzel sticks, graham crackers, marshmallows, banana or pineapple chunks, cups of water, plates, wet wipes

TEACHING TIPS

Be aware of food allergies when providing snacks for preschoolers. Provide alternate foods as needed.

If your kids travel to the Super Snacks site for their snacks, you may want to choose another activity instead of Stand Up Snack.

STEP 3 Use one or more of these activities to help children *identify ways they can stand up and do right for Jesus.*

QUICKSTEP: WHEEL OF LIFE GAME

Before class, print out the Wheel of Life game from the resources CD. You'll need a copy for each child.

Even though you are young, you can be heroes for Jesus in your life *(point to each on the game card)* **by saying kind words** *(mouth)*, **by trusting God** *(Bible)*, **by doing loving actions** *(heart)*, **and by thinking good thoughts** *(thought balloon)*—**just as we learned in our Bible Memory.** Show children the Wheel of Life game. Let them color the wheel. Demonstrate how to play the game. Stand a pencil on its point in the center of the wheel. Drop a large paper clip over the pencil. Hold the pencil with one hand and spin the paper clip with your other hand. Younger children may need help with this. Wherever the paper clip lands, have each child tell one thing he will do to be a hero for Jesus in that area of life.

OPTION 1: STAND UP SNACK

Have children clean their hands. Give each child a plate, a graham cracker, a handful of pretzel sticks, a few marshmallows, and fruit. Show children how they can stick the pretzels into the marshmallows and fruit. Help them use the snack items to build a structure that can stand up. Encourage them to use the graham crackers as a foundation for their structures.

Let children tell you about their structures before they gobble them up. As you enjoy the snack with the children, say: **The graham crackers were a sturdy foundation for your snack structures. They provided a flat surface to hold everything steady so the snack wouldn't fall down. We have a foundation for our lives, just like these graham crackers are the foundation for our snack. It's Jesus! In our time at VBS, we've learned how much Jesus loves us. We can be heroes for Jesus by trusting Him, serving Him, and helping others to know about Him. Let's thank Him for our food and for the new friends we have made at VBS.**

Lead children in prayer. Invite children to pray if they want to.

OPTION 2: STAND UP STUDENTS

Before class, print out the boy and girl figures onto card stock. Or use regular paper and mount the figures. They need to be stiff in order to stand up. Cut the figures out. Remove and throw away the wire clips from the binder clips.

Show children the figures. Set out crayons or markers and have children color the figures to represent themselves. Help children slide their finished figures into the binder clips, making them into stands. When everyone is finished, gather the children with their figures.

Let's use our figures to think about some ways children can stand up and do right for Jesus. Stand your figure up if I say a way you can do right for Jesus. Lay your figure down if I say something that's not doing right.

- **Pushing someone out of the way so you can be first in line**
- **Asking, "May I have a turn?" when you want a friend's toy**
- **Talking loudly to your friend while the teacher is telling the Bible story**
- **Helping your mom or dad carry the groceries**
- **Singing "Jesus Loves Me"**
- **Telling a friend, "I'm not your friend anymore."**
- **Hitting your younger brother or sister**
- **Hugging your brother or sister**
- **Obeying your parents**

Continue the game as long as children are interested and you have ideas. Children can add their own ideas too. If time allows, let the children play with their figures for a few minutes.

Remember to stand up and do what's right for Jesus! You can do it! Sing "Stand Up!" from the CD.

MATERIALS

large binder clips, *Teaching Resources CD* Track 1 and CD Session 5 boy and girl patterns, crayons or washable markers, scissors, CD player

TEACHING TIP

Children will love to play with these personalized figures. If you have access to a digital camera and printer, take full-body photographs of the children earlier in VBS. Instead of using the boy and girl figures, let children create figures using their own photographs for this activity.

PreSchool Teacher 45

SESSION 5

LIFE FOCUS: Heroes stand for TRUTH!

MATERIALS
none

TEACHING TIP
You may want to invite parents to join you for the last few minutes of this session. Children can sing this song and say the Bible Memory to show what they've learned at VBS.

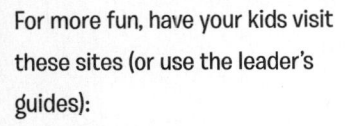

For more fun, have your kids visit these sites (or use the leader's guides):
- **Power Projects**—Choose from a variety of creative and purposeful projects and activities that will help kids remember to be heroes who save the day!
- **Super Snacks**—Kids will love making and eating these tasty snacks that reinforce the Bible story.
- **Action Games**—Give kids time to move, play, work on hero skills, and relax. All the super fun activities connect to the Bible hero story and Bible focus.

STEP 4
Use this activity to help each child *choose a way to be a hero who does what is right.*

QUICKSTEP: SIT DOWN, STAND UP SONG

Teach children this song, to the tune of "Row, Row, Row Your Boat." Have children sit down and jump up as the song directs. For added fun, have children hold their shields as they sing.

**Sit down, sit down,
everybody scrunch up tight.
Jump up, jump up,
everybody do what's right.**

More verses:
. . . if you said your prayers last night.
. . . love your God with all your might.

Today we learned about a young man who spoke up and saved his Uncle Paul. Paul loved God with all his might! We can love God with all our might too. At VBS we've learned that we can do great things for Jesus no matter what size or age we are. Remember to do what's right, and you'll be a hero for Jesus your whole life long!

Ask children for other ideas of how they can be heroes and do what is right. **I want you to tell me one way you will act like a hero by doing something that is right.** Continue to sing the song as children wait for their parents or closing assembly.

From the *PreSchool Teaching Resources CD* Session 5 printable file
- Add your own news or leave as is and print copies of the **Hero HeadQuarters Family Page**. It lets parents know what their kids are learning and gives an overview of the Bible story, as well as suggests ways they can encourage their children to be heroes, saving the day!
- Print copies of **A Boy Shares His Food Puzzle** onto card stock. Kids will love making puzzles to take home. Have a supply of envelopes handy for them to put their puzzle pieces in.
- Print copies of **A Boy Shares His Food Coloring Page** for kids to take home and color with their friends and families.

Coloring Fun

with familiar Bible stories from Genesis to Revelation

A great inexpensive gift for each child in your family or classroom!

Children will enjoy coloring the simple drawings of familiar Bible stories from both the Old and New Testaments and will learn about the Bible as they color.

- 45 favorite stories
- Over 380 pages of coloring fun
- Bible references on every page
- Perforated pages make it easy to use

The Gigantic Coloring Book of Bible Stories

Only **$4.99** each

For more information or to order visit
www.standardpub.com
or call **1-800-543-1353**

Standard PUBLISHING
Bringing The Word to Life

THE ADULTS ARE HERE FOR SMALL GROUP
BUT WHAT DO WE DO WITH THE KIDS?!

Relax—we've got you covered. Just add one adult or teenage leader to these easy-to-lead sessions to keep kids engaged, entertained, and growing in their faith! While parents are meeting, gather elementary-age kids together and dive in. Each session is:

- **FLEXIBLE**—adaptable for 2 to 12 children
- **MULTI-AGED**—because you're never sure who'll show up
- **LOW-PREP**—using supplies from your kitchen, office, or garage
- **45 MINUTES OF FUN**—with time-stretchers to fill an hour
- Less than **$1 PER SESSION**!

The Small Group Solutions for Kids series is perfect for:

- Adult small groups
- House church
- Sunday school
- Evening programs in smaller churches

13 VERY COOL STORIES and Why Jesus Told Them
ITEM # 41221

13 VERY BAD DAYS and How God Fixed Them
ITEM # 41220

Standard PUBLISHING
Bringing The Word to Life

Available at your local Christian bookstore or **www.standardpub.com**